PRISONS

in Crisis

PRISONS
in Crisis

William L. Selke

INDIANA UNIVERSITY PRESS
Bloomington and Indianapolis

The paper used in this publication meets the minimum requirements of
American National Standard for Information Sciences—Permanence of
Paper for Printed Library Materials, ANSI Z39.48-1984.

∞™

Manufactured in the United States of America

Library of Congress Cataloging-in-Publication Data

Selke, William L.
    Prisons in crisis / William L. Selke.
        p. cm.
    Includes bibliographical references and index.
        ISBN 0-253-35149-9 (cloth : alk. paper). — ISBN 0-253-20814-9
    (paper : alk. paper)
        1. Prisons. 2. Prisons—United States. 3. Corrections.
    4. Corrections—United States. I. Title.
    HV8982.S45 1993
    365'.973—dc20   92-42807

1 2 3 4 5   97 96 95 94 93

Dedicated to Virginia and Albert Selke, for all they taught me and especially what they did not teach. One could not ask for better parents.

In its intention, I am well convinced
that the prison is kind, humane and
meant for reformation; but I am
persuaded that those benevolent
gentlemen who carry it into execution,
do not know what it is they are doing.

I believe that very few men are capable
of estimating the immense amount of
torture and agony which this dreadful
punishment, prolonged for years, inflicts
upon the sufferers; and in guessing at it
myself, and in reasoning from what I
have seen on their faces, and what to
my certain knowledge they feel within, I
am only the more convinced that there
is a depth of terrible endurance in it
which none but the sufferers themselves
can fathom, and which no man has a
right to inflict upon his fellow creature.

Charles Dickens, 1842

Contents

Figures and Tables

Preface

This book is about the futility of using prisons to deal with nonviolent criminal offenders. Of course, no responsible person would advocate leaving the violent murderer, rapist, or child molester free to roam about in society. Prison is very effective in segregating this group of criminals. However, our addiction to prison as a panacea for all social problems is beginning to outstrip our ability to pay. The public may not like it. And politicians will miss it as a campaign tool. But the "lock 'em up and throw away the key" approach to dealing with crime has run its course. It is counterproductive to use the prison sanction with those who do not pose a direct threat to society. In the words of Oscar Wilde,

> The vilest deeds like poison weeds,
> bloom well in prison air.
> It is only what is good in Man,
> that wastes and withers there.

Critics will say that prison reform is too costly, too risky, and too impractical. But their arguments begin to sound uninformed as we better understand the prison situation. Unlike most of the major social problems we face today, ignoring the prison problem does not save money but rather costs us billions of dollars annually. And more importantly, it threatens to bring chaos and anarchy to our system of justice. Prison overcrowding requires us to release certain inmates early and to reject taking other convicted offenders simply because there is no more room. This haphazard situation with regard to prison release and entry is much more dangerous and threatening to public safety than a planned approach for dealing with nonviolent offenders in the community, which would save prison space for those who need to be segregated. Lastly, what is impractical is expecting that we can subject nonviolent offenders to years of degradation and brutality in prison and then release them telling them to "walk the chalk line." They are angry, bitter, frustrated, and unprepared to reenter society.

In this book we will attempt to understand how the acute problem of prison overcrowding came about and what might be done to address this nagging social issue. The matter can no longer be ignored. It is beginning to place severe strains on many state budgets. As we will see in table 2.2, nearly every state is under some kind of court order to address problems of prison overcrowding and inhumane conditions. Funding to build and operate prisons is siphoning off scarce funds from education, health care, and environmental protection.

In some states there are prisoners sleeping in tents, and in other states new prisons have been built but they stand empty because there is no money to run them. Prison funding is the fastest growing segment of most state budgets. Riots and hostage incidents are becoming increasingly common in the prisons, posing serious danger to those bedraggled employees in the field of corrections. When we consider that the average cost of holding one inmate in prison for one year is well over twenty-thousand dollars, the question must be raised as to whether we cannot find more positive ways to spend correctional funds.

Prisons in Crisis has as its major theme that effective management of prisons can only take place when the sanction of imprisonment is utilized in a more circumspect and systematic manner. There are many other sentences that can be used successfully with nonviolent offenders. An underlying theme in each of the chapters is that prison sentences are best reserved for the violent and dangerous offenders while the network of community correctional programs is improved to better serve those convicted of property crimes and public order offenses. The basic reason for limiting the use of prisons is simply that they are not achieving their goals although they are extremely expensive to operate. Talk of treatment has almost been abandoned in corrections. And the high percentage of inmates who return to prison suggests that prisons are not achieving much in the way of deterrence, either. Yet the dismal failures of prisons continue to be rewarded with higher and higher levels of funding.

One of the unique features of the book is the detailed consideration of comparative and international corrections. In particular, there is a strong emphasis on Scandinavian criminology and correctional philosophies as they are practiced in Denmark. This body of literature provides an interesting contrast to the field of corrections in the United States. Scandinavian prison systems are recognized throughout the world as being models based on the most progressive principles of penology. The criminologists in Denmark, Sweden, and Norway have played an important role in defining the basic values and practices that lead to a more effective system of justice. There is a moderation of punishment in these systems that is indeed indicative of a kinder and gentler society. We will see that the Scandinavian philosophy of prison use is a reflection of broader social values that emphasize respect for human dignity with opportunity and support for all citizens.

Another important feature of the book is its policy orientation with an interdisciplinary nature. Throughout the following pages there will be examples of research and theory from a number of different fields, including sociology, law, anthropology, psychology, political science, history, and social work, along with criminology and criminal justice. Also included will be discussions of writings from many other nations. It is hoped that the interdisciplinary materials along with the cross-cultural perspectives of those from outside U.S. borders will provide an interesting and unique framework which can be used to better understand the problems of our prisons and the possibilities for making them better. A policy orientation suggests that we attempt to put forth ideas and recommendations for prison reform that are within the constraints and realities of the political process and modern-day society.

The focus of *Prisons in Crisis* will be on adult male prisons, since these are the places where most of the nation's prisoners are held. However, women's prisons, juvenile institutions, county jails, and other correctional facilities face many of the same basic problems. Prisons in the United States have never before been so overcrowded, understaffed, and under fire. The first chapter of the book will analyze the skyrocketing prison populations and compare the rates of imprisonment across the fifty states, as well as the rates of countries around the world. It will also contain a discussion of the ideologies and attitudes that provide rationale for the use of prisons. Chapter 2 presents a glimpse at the nature of prison life today through a review of some of the extensive court cases that have addressed the issue of prisoners' rights. In addition we will look in some detail at the nature of recent prison litigation, which has become more concerned with overcrowding and general prison conditions. Contained in chapter 3 is a presentation of Scandinavian criminology, including the principles that form the foundation of the correctional philosophy. The prison system of Denmark will be discussed in some depth in order to illustrate the potential for developing purposeful and effective institutions.

Chapter 4 is devoted to comparing and contrasting the traditional closed model of imprisonment with the open model that characterizes the Scandinavian system. The chapter also includes a procedure for creating a "prison index" that would allow us to measure the relative conditions of different prisons and compare the effects of different kinds of prison environments. In chapter 5 attention is directed to the many programs and policies from nations around the globe that have had a positive impact on improving the delivery of correctional services. It may still be possible to learn from the experiences of others. The contents of chapter 6 include an examination of some of the most interesting proposals that have been put forth for dealing with prisons in crisis along with comments regarding the feasibility of actually implementing such changes in our system of justice. Finally, the historical principles of corrections are presented in an effort to demonstrate that the basic elements of prison reform and social justice are already in place. The question remains whether we have the political courage and moral conviction to follow them.

Acknowledgments

My thanks to the many friends and colleagues at Indiana University and elsewhere whose thoughts and comments were very influential during the writing of this book. John Smykla was especially helpful with his comments on the manuscript, and Paul Jesilow, Steen Andersson, Ed McGarrell, Hal Pepinsky, and Bill Head have provided much "food for thought" in our many discussions and debates over the years. I would also like to acknowledge the kindness and expertise of Judy Kelley and Gina Doglione who helped make the preparation of these materials much less stressful. All of the people at the University of Copenhagen were most generous with their time, and they assisted me significantly in beginning to understand the culture of Denmark and the Scandinavian perspective. Finally, I would like to express my love and gratitude to Beth, Emily, and Hank Selke who provide the kind of family support and pleasant atmosphere that make writing easy.

1. The Sentence of Imprisonment

Prison Populations

There is widespread agreement that one of the most pressing issues in the field of criminal justice during the 1990s will be prison overcrowding. The Department of Justice (1989) reports that the increases in prison populations since 1973 have been "by far the most dramatic" in the history of prisons in the United States. In fact, every year during the 1980s there were increases in imprisonment rates to the point where the number of prison inmates is now over 300% of what it was in the early seventies. Figure 1.1 clearly illustrates the dramatic nature of increases in prison populations during this period. It must also be remembered that these figures do not even include the large numbers of juveniles who are placed in public and private institutions, the thousands who are detained in county jails, and those serving time in hundreds of facilities such as halfway houses and work release centers. Altogether, there are well over a million persons locked up in the U.S. correctional system, and it is estimated that we now spend more than fifty billion dollars each year to arrest, prosecute, and punish criminal offenders (Lindren, 1987).

Explanations for this trend toward greater punitiveness have varied. On the one hand, there are those who suggest that the public may have an "unconstrained appetite for criminal punishments" (Zimmerman et al., 1988, 148). Their research suggests that public opinion supports the imprisonment of more people for longer periods of time. Within the current political climate, it does appear that there is little tolerance for reductions and reforms in the use of prisons. On the other hand, Gottfredson and Taylor (1984) conclude that policymakers misperceive the public will. They present

Figure 1.1 Number of Sentenced State and
Federal Prisoners, Year-End, 1925-1990

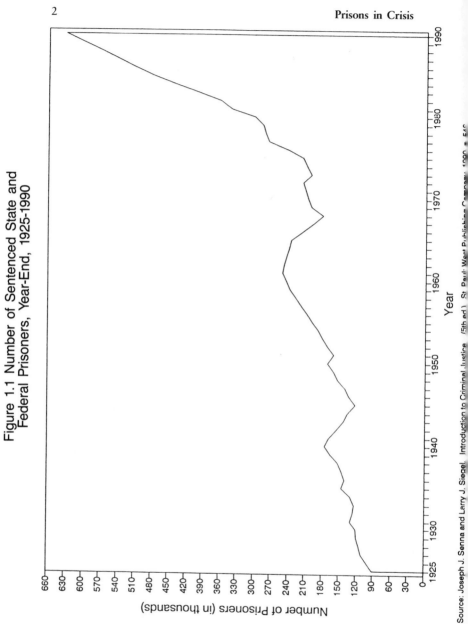

Number of Prisoners (in thousands)

Year

Source: Joseph J. Senna and Larry J. Siegel, Introduction to Criminal Justice, (5th ed.), St. Paul: West Publishing Company, 1990, p. 546.

data and argue that the public *is* willing to support various nonpunitive goals such as rehabilitation, perhaps to a greater extent than policymakers. Thus, it is not clear as to who is pushing whom toward more stringent criminal sanctions. The debate about whether public opinion or officials' attitudes determine the rate of imprisonment is but one of many possible explanations for our increasingly punitive society.

Another type of explanation for the rises in imprisonment rates has to do with the importance of various social and demographic variables as they influence sentencing practices. Zimring and Hawkins (1991) reviewed some of the recent theories that have been put forth to explain the prison binge. Of course, it has always been assumed that imprisonment rates are influenced primarily by the crime rates. According to the rational model of the justice system, more crime leads to more arrests and prosecutions which, in turn, result in more people going to prison and higher rates of incarceration. Similarly, less crime would result in fewer arrests and prosecutions with correspondingly lower imprisonment rates. This view of the justice process, however, is based on an overly simplistic conception of the legal system, and it exaggerates the relationship between crime and imprisonment rates. Mullin (1980), for example, came to the conclusion that there is no consistent relationship between crime rates and imprisonment rates. There is some evidence that violent crime rates have an influence on imprisonment rates (see Carroll and Doubet, 1983). But even this relationship is not a direct and simple one. When we consider the matter of economics and unemployment, it appears that these factors may also influence prison rates indirectly through their impact on crime rates. With higher levels of unemployment and lower levels of financial stability, the likelihood of criminal behavior is enhanced. Indeed, the research by Jankovic (1977) concluded that unemployment rates directly influence prison rates. It has often been argued that one of the underlying functions of corrections in modern capitalistic society is to control surplus labor through the incarceration of certain groups of untrained and undereducated individuals.

In a related article by McGarrell (1991), demographic variables were examined to determine their relative influence on incarceration rates. He considered the relative effects on prison rates of several factors, including the level of urbanization, industrialization, unemployment, racial differentiation and inequality, available state revenue, percentage black population, and violent crime rate. His most significant conclusion was that states with higher percentages of black citizens adopt harsher imprisonment policies *even when there is not a higher rate of violent crime.* This kind of finding must make us pause to consider the possibility that institutional racism at the structural level is an important determinant of higher prison rates. And finally, it should be kept in mind that a wide range of policy decisions also exert major pressures on the imprisonment rate. Legal and correctional policies on matters such as determinate sentencing, good time laws, parole and revocation, mandatory sentences, habitual offender laws, and pretrial detention clearly influence the number of individuals spending time and the amount of time spent.

The reason there is so much interest and speculation about the forces that determine imprisonment rates is that there is so much variation among different nations around the world, as well as among the different states of our nation. If rates of incarceration were fairly similar across different cultures or fairly consistent among the fifty states, we might conclude that there is some reasoned consensus as to proper levels of punishment and that our criminal justice policies are carried out in a relatively consistent and equitable manner. When we discover very large differences in imprisonment rates, however, two basic questions beg for our attention. How do different jurisdictions end up with very different levels of punishment if crime levels are not that different? This is what the discussion above is all about. The second question is one that deals with the issue of fairness. Is the likelihood and severity of a life-threatening prison sentence determined in large measure by where one happens to be arrested, convicted, and sentenced? As will be seen in the following section, the answer to the latter question is a clear and definite "yes."

Comparisons of Imprisonment Rates

Differences among Nations

Although it is common to hear that our nation is lenient in its dealings with offenders, figure 1.2 shows that this is certainly not

Figure 1.2 Comparison
of International Imprisonment Rates

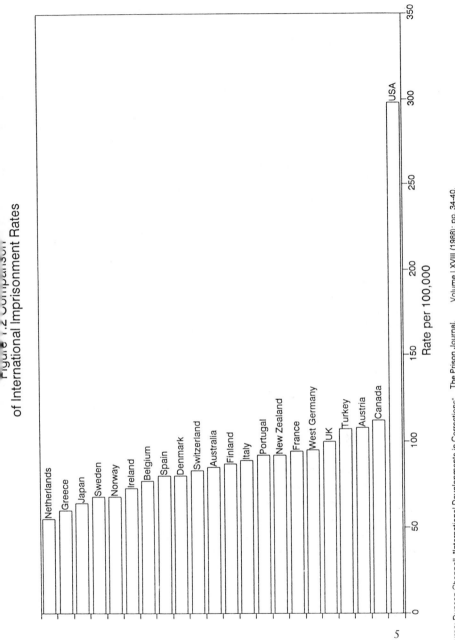

Rate per 100,000

Source: Duncan Chappell. "International Developments in Corrections".   The Prison Journal.   Volume LXVIII (1988): pp. 34-40.

the case in comparison with the other major industrialized, democratic countries. These data from the Australian Institute on Criminology graphically portray the wide variations among the twenty-two modern nations. The rate of imprisonment in the United States is nearly three times as great as that in Canada, which is the second most punitive nation. The U.S. rate is approximately ten times that of the Netherlands. These findings are consistent with statistics collected in earlier studies. For instance, Doleschal (1977) reached the same conclusion over a decade ago in stating that the United States had the highest and the Netherlands the lowest imprisonment rates in the world.

In similar analyses of international imprisonment rates, Waller and Chan (1974) and Biles (1979) reached comparable conclusions regarding the status of the United States in terms of imprisonment rates. The only countries that have appeared to have had rates of incarceration in the same approximate range as the United States are South Africa and the former Soviet Union. It could probably be expected that certain other totalitarian and fascist nations have rates as high or higher than the United States, but these governments are not likely to participate in the kind of research that addresses questions about how citizens are treated within their legal systems. Nevertheless, the United States occupies a position that clearly places it among the most punitive countries in the world.

Ranking the Fifty States

It is perhaps understandable that very large differences exist in rates among nations because of their very diverse histories, traditions, and cultures. This matter will be addressed later in chapter 3. Within our own country, however, we could expect there to be some degree of uniformity and consistency across the states. Recent research by Austin and Tillman (1988) indicates that there is as much variation among the fifty states as there is among nations around the world. Table 1.1 contains the Austin and Tillman rankings of the fifty states and Washington, D.C., using simple imprisonment rates for each state and imprisonment rates divided by arrest rates. In dividing by arrest rates, the authors attempt to control for the amount of crime in the various states. Also presented in the table are the comparable rankings from a similar piece of research (Selke and Andersson, 1992). These rankings were obtained through the use of a more sophisticated method in which data were transformed into logarithms and a regression analysis was undertaken to control for reported crime rates (and arrest rates, although these were not significant). The primary rankings in column A then represent the differences in imprisonment rates among the states *after* we have removed the crime levels as possible explanations for the variations. The quotient used for the primary ranking indicates the simple percentage of reported crime that results in the handing down of a prison sentence.

Several interesting observations can be made regarding table 1.1. First and foremost, it is obvious that even after controlling for crime rates, there are major differences in the levels of imprisonment around the nation. The states with the lowest rankings were far less punitive than those at the other end of the scale. Among the most punitive states, such as Alabama, Mississippi, and Nevada, the levels of punitiveness are 300%–400% greater than those of states at the top of the table like Minnesota and Utah. It is important for us to remember that these differences exist even after we have controlled for crime rates. These data provide strong evidence that the levels of crime are not closely related to prison rates as it is typically assumed. This means that there is a great deal of discretion and disparity in the use of prison sanctions; *states and communities are very inconsistent in the use of prison sanctions.*

We also notice in table 1.1 that there is a high degree of consistency in the rankings of states regardless of what methods are used. Whether using the simple imprisonment rates (column B) and simple prisoner / arrest ratios (column C) or regression data with controls for crime rates (column A), arrest rates (column D) or crime and arrest rates (column E), the results are similar. For example, there are five states that are among the ten least punitive in all columns—Minnesota, Rhode Island, Utah, North Dakota, and Massachusetts. Washington and Colorado are among the ten least punitive states in four of the five columns. The situation is similar on the other end of the scale. Alabama, Nevada, South Carolina, Delaware, and Louisiana are among the ten most punitive states on all scales. Georgia and Arkansas are also found toward the punitive end of the scale in each column.

Another important matter that becomes obvious is the geographical distribution of states on the punitiveness scale. At the punitive

Table 1.1. Rankings of the Punitiveness of States

	A		Quotient	B Austin-Tillman[1]	C Austin-Tillman[2]	D Rank[3]	E Rank[4]
Rank	State		Quotient	Austin-Tillman[1]	Austin-Tillman[2]	Rank[3]	Rank[4]
1.	Minnesota	MN	0.01300	ND	MN	MN	MN
2.	Rhode Island	RI	0.01892	MN	UT	ND	UT
3.	Washington	WA	0.01910	WV	ND	UT	ND
4.	Utah	UT	0.01958	NH	CT	CT	WA
5.	North Dakota	ND	0.02012	VT	WI	WI	RI
6.	Vermont	VT	0.02131	RI	CO	CO	CO
7.	Massachusetts	MA	0.02155	IA	WA	WA	MA
8.	Colorado	CO	0.02248	MA	RI	RI	HI
9.	New Hampshire	NH	0.02402	ME	NM	MA	CT
10.	Hawaii	HI	0.02424	UT	MA	NH	NM
11.	Iowa	IA	0.02439	NE	HI	NM	VT
12.	New Mexico	NM	0.02658	WI	IA	IA	IA
13.	Oregon	OR	0.02870	WA	ME	HI	NH
14.	Connecticut	CT	0.02882	PA	NH	WV	WI
15.	Nebraska	NE	0.02977	HI	NE	ME	OR
16.	Texas	TX	0.02991	CT	MT	NE	NE
17.	Maine	ME	0.03001	ID	KY	MT	ME
18.	Wisconsin	WI	0.03022	CO	ID	KY	FL
19.	Florida	FL	0.03116	KY	WV	ID	MT
20.	Illinois	IL	0.03157	MT	OR	VT	TX
21.	Montana[5]	MT	0.03196	TN	IL	OR	IL
22.	Tennessee	TN	0.03344	SD	VT	PA	ID
23.	New Jersey	NJ	0.03364	IL	PA	IL	CA
24.	Idaho	ID	0.03465	NM	CA	TN	TN
25.	West Virginia	WV	0.03515	NJ	TN	CA	NJ
26.	California	CA	0.03550	WY	AK	NJ	WV
27.	New York	NY	0.03847	IN	AZ	SD	AZ
28.	Michigan	MI	0.04011	OR	FL	FL	NY
29.	Arizona	AZ	0.04271	VA	NJ	AZ	KY
30.	Pennsylvania	PA	0.04299	MO	SD	AK	PA
31.	Kentucky[6]	KY	0.04495	OH	TX	TX	MI
32.	Missouri	MO	0.04631	AR	NY	NY	MO
33.	Indiana	IN	0.04660	NY	MO	MO	KS
34.	Wyoming	WY	0.04713	CA	MS	MS	IN
35.	Kansas	KS	0.04751	TX	NC	KS	MD
36.	Ohio	OH	0.04787	KS	KS	NC	OH
37.	Georgia	GA	0.04869	NC	MD	MD	WY
38.	Oklahoma	OK	0.04912	MS	IN	IN	NC
39.	Maryland	MD	0.05148	MI	VA	VA	AK
40.	Arkansas	AR	0.05347	FL	OH	OH	OK
41.	North Carolina	NC	0.05376	GA	LA	WY	AR
42.	Virginia	VA	0.05480	MD	WY	AR	VA
43.	Louisiana	LA	0.05891	OK	NV	MI	GA
44.	South Dakota	SD	0.05975	AL	AR	LA	LA
45.	Alaska	AK	0.06304	AZ	MI	NV	SD
46.	Delaware	DE	0.06601	DE	DE	DE	NV

Table 1.1.—Continued

	A			B	C	D	E
				Austin-Tillman[1]	Austin-Tillman[2]		
Rank	State		Quotient	Austin-Tillman[1]	Austin-Tillman[2]	Rank[3]	Rank[4]
47.	South Carolina	SC	0.06664	AK	OK	OK	MS
48.	Nevada	NV	0.06780	SC	GA	GA	DE
49.	Alabama	AL	0.06897	LA	SC	SC	SC
50.	Mississippi	MS	0.07445	NV	AL	AL	AL
51.	Washington	DC	0.10708	DC	DC	DC	DC

1. Ranking based on simple imprisonment rates for 1987 updating the Austin and Tillman ranking for 1985.

2. Ranking based on the quotient imprisonment rate / arrest rate for 1987 corresponding to Austin and Tillman's prisoner / arrest ratio ranking for 1985.

3. Ranking based on corrected residuals in the regression analysis with imprisonment rate as the dependent variable and arrest rate as the independent variable.

4. Ranking based on corrected residuals in the regression analysis with imprisonment rate as the dependent variable and crime rate *and* arrest rate as independent variables.

5. Arrest data were not available for Montana in 1987. The arrest rate was calculated by averaging arrest and population estimates from 1986 and 1988.

6. Arrest data for Kentucky were unavailable for 1987 and 1988. The arrest rate was projected by using arrests and population estimates from 1985 and 1986.

end of the scale, we find primarily states from the South, while the states ranked as least punitive tend to be those in the North and Northeast. One explanation for this trend might be related to the findings mentioned earlier regarding the racial aspect of punitiveness. Since the Southern states tend to have a larger percentage of minority residents compared to most of the rest of the nation, this demographic variable may indeed be important in explaining the large variations in punitiveness. Furthermore, it has often been claimed that there may exist a conservative "Southern mentality" that breeds an ideology more favorable to punishment and harsh criminal sanctions. Attitudes and beliefs about the causes of crime and ideologies regarding how to deal with crime are central in our attempts to understand the legal system. This matter of ideology is a topic that needs to be explored in greater detail. In the section below, an effort will be made to analyze the ideological dilemmas that are inherent in criminal justice. Elements of different ideologies, or underlying belief systems, are held by those who work in the justice system and tend to support or oppose the use of imprisonment to varying degrees (see Selke, 1980).

Ideologies and Criminal Justice

There are several competing ideologies in the field of criminal justice. The punishment ideology has been dominant in the legal system and is the underlying premise for the use of imprisonment on a large scale. A punishment orientation is based on the principles of classical criminology and the assumptions that people are rational and their behaviors are a matter of choice or "free will." From this viewpoint, the ultimate objective of the justice system is to hand out punishments so that potential criminal offenders will learn that the consequences of their behavior will outweigh the benefits of the crime. Knowing this, rational individuals will decide not to commit criminal acts. The classical criminologist will contend that if we "let the punishment fit the crime," then offenders will be deterred. Those who have been convicted of crimes will be deterred by the harshness of the prison sentences (specific deterrence), and others who contemplate committing a crime will soon learn that "crime does not pay" (general deterrence). The more certain the punishment, the greater will be the deterrent value.

As for the use of prisons, their importance in the classical scheme has been achieved because of the supposed fear and dread of a prison sentence. Some initial doubts, however, can be raised about the seeming simplicity of the classical model. There is first a problem with the assumption of rationality. Of course, we all hope that we ourselves and others behave in a fairly rational manner most of the time, and we probably do. But everyone behaves irrationally on one occasion or another, and often these are the precise occasions when crimes are committed. Also, to make arrests and punishments certain is an impossible task. How many police officers would be needed to guarantee that ALL criminal offenders were caught and arrested? In addition, when we resort too quickly to the harsher punishments like prison, we eventually make all lesser punishments seem unimportant. Then there are also those who, far from being scared or deterred by the threat of prison, will see it as a challenge and a status symbol. So while the classical ideology may be appealing since it does sound like good common sense, it is not so simple to use in the real world.

The other major competing ideology in the U.S. justice system during this century has been the treatment or rehabilitation perspective. Based on positive criminology, the treatment ideology assumes that people commit crimes because of some underlying problem. The problem may be seen as chemical, biological, genetic, emotional, intellectual, or social. It is the ultimate objective of the justice system to diagnose the problem and develop an appropriate treatment plan. From the positive perspective, criminal behavior is viewed as a pathology or a "sickness" and the medical model is the foundation upon which to build effective treatment approaches. While the use of prison is not as basic to the treatment ideology as it is to the ideology of punishment, it has not been viewed as antithetical. Treatment specialists have been eager to try new methods in any variety of settings including the prison. Indeed, there has been one line of thought that has suggested the best environment for treatment and rehabilitation was the prison because of the high level of control that a therapist could exert over a prison inmate.

Criticisms of the treatment ideology have not been scarce either. There has always been a skepticism about the effectiveness of most treatments with most kinds of clients, not only criminal offenders. A closely related concern has been the difficulty in defining when treatment has been successful, particularly in the case of prisoners when the practical meaning of "rehabilitated" means the person will not commit further crimes. Obviously, we cannot make this type of prediction about future behaviors with a very high degree of certainty. There is an additional criticism of the treatment ideology that deals with the methods of treatment. It is clear that certain "treatments" such as drug therapy and electroshock can change behavior in dramatic (and often unpredictable) ways, but such intrusive techniques are usually not considered appropriate for the majority of prisoners who are nonviolent offenders. Finally, there has been widespread concern regarding the misuse and stigma of pathological terms like "antisocial" and "psychopathic" in describing offenders.

A third major ideology in criminal justice has been loosely referred to as critical criminology. While not as systematic and detailed as the two older, traditional schools of criminology, the critical perspective has emerged as an alternative approach to understanding and dealing with criminal behavior. This viewpoint has generated a number of questions about the basic tenets of both the punitive and treatment ideologies. Most of the concerns just discussed have been raised by those who might consider themselves critical criminologists. Prison reform is one of the matters that has been of utmost importance from the critical perspective, and this issue illustrates the problems associated with an alternative ideology. Prison reform is usually met with resistance from all sides and generally has not enjoyed much popularity. From a conservative political standpoint, prison reform activities are seen as attempts to encourage the "coddling of criminals." These critics argue that we need more severe punishments and prisons that are more frightening in order to achieve the aim of deterrence. The neoclassical philosophy of today holds that retribution, incapacitation, and deterrence (through the use of prisons) are the only realistic and attainable goals for the criminal justice system.

From a liberal political perspective, it is often argued that improving prison conditions will guarantee continued overuse. There is, of course, some risk that those involved in studying and researching prisons will be coopted and consciously or perhaps subconsciously contribute to the perpetuation of prison networks. Furthermore, there is the criticism that by focusing on the immediate problems of imprisonment we are ignoring the more basic issues of social injustice. Then there is the resistance to reform from within the correctional system itself. Because of pressures from inside and outside, prison authorities have not been amenable to suggestions for significant change and improvement.

The critical ideology, however, has been influential in generating some important concepts that challenge the rationale for many imprisonment policies. The entire criminal justice system is affected by the expanded use of prison. Because of the severity of lengthy prison terms, there is an unnecessary tension created at each decision point within the justice process. Given the current situation, it is important that criminologists and others with common concerns about the harshness and arbitrariness of prison sanctions present alternative ways of thinking about crime causation and crime control. Schur (1980) reviewed many of the older theories and research studies that have contributed significantly to an emerging ideology about crime and punishment that is less focused on the punishment and/or treatment models of criminal justice. For example, the theory of "drift" put forth by Matza (1964) has continued to challenge the commonly accepted "pathology-corrections" philosophy of crime causation and crime control by suggesting that offenders do not necessarily choose and are not necessarily driven but commit crimes somewhat by happenstance. They drift into criminal activities. The related research on "labeling" theory has also served to shift the emphasis away from the naive focus on single-factor theories of individual problems toward a recognition of the sociolegal construction of crime (Becker, 1968). There may be something of a self-fulfilling prophecy when one is labeled as a "deviant" or "criminal." Similarly, the concept of "secondary deviance" discussed by Lofland (1966) provided insight into the potentially crime-producing results that derive from the processing and stigmatization by the justice system.

There are other works with major implications for crime control ideology that deal with the meaning of crime statistics, the scope of the criminal law, and the political nature of crime definitions. For example, Kitsuse and Cicourel (1963) demonstrated that the compilation of crime statistics reflects only the practices and procedures of the criminal justice system and law enforcement agencies rather than providing a measure of the actual extent of crime. They thus challenged the widely accepted notion that crime is now and always on the rise. The early works of Sutherland (1949) illustrated the reservations of society to criminalize white-collar crimes that many considered to be socially harmful. Obversely, the tendency to criminalize behaviors that many consider not harmful, including victimless crimes, has been examined in some detail (e.g., Packer, 1968). Finally, the sociocultural and political contexts of criminal definitions and crime control policies have been critically examined, providing a better understanding of the inevitable political biases and class conflicts that are manifested in the law and the criminal justice system (see Chambliss, 1964; Platt, 1969; Quinney, 1970; Pepinsky, 1980).

All of the above writings are similar in that they offer very different approaches to understanding and responding to criminal behavior. There have also been a few writings in the specific area of corrections that have provided uniquely different views about the meaning and use of imprisonment. For the most part, research on prisons and prisoners has been based on traditional assumptions and has provided little meaningful knowledge about the use and necessity of the prison sanction. Certain works, however, have provided useful information for combating the simplistic and often uninformed beliefs regarding the value of imprisonment. One of the most important contributions to understanding the personal impact of institutionalization was the widely read article by Garfinkel (1956) describing what he termed the "degradation ceremonies." This discussion of the humiliation and dehumanization that results from public denunciations as exemplified by the use of imprisonment was a very significant departure from the recently popular myths about rehabilitation in prisons. In addition, Mitford's (1973) scathing critique of the prison system has been most useful in countering the widespread criticisms of our "country club" prisons. Another important book along the same lines was that of Murton and Hyams (1969). This latter work not only presents a lucid description of one state's prison system, but also documents why it is so difficult to bring about any meaningful change, given the political, economic, and bureaucratic realities of corrections.

Together, the above writings have cast serious doubt on the rehabilitative justification for imprisonment. Perhaps more importantly, other studies have challenged the assumption that the use of imprisonment serves as a deterrent. The research on general deterrence theory is not conclusive, and most of that body of literature has concentrated on the deterrent value of capital punishment. But even the support for capital punishment as a deterrent has been limited (e.g., Ehrlich, 1975). There is, however, a large body of literature in which no empirical support is found for the deterrent value of criminal sanctions (see, for example, Tittle, 1969; Chiricos and Waldo, 1970; Logan, 1972; Bailey et al., 1974; Sjoquist, 1973; Pogue, 1975; Forst, 1976; Blumstein et al., 1978; Tittle, 1980). Two of the leading researchers in this area have concluded after reviewing the extensive body of literature that there is *not* currently consistent empirical support for the general deterrent value of legal sanctions (Tittle and Logan, 1973).

With little research support for the rehabilitative and deterrent functions of prison, we are left with the justification known as incapacitation. There can be no doubt that when people are imprisoned, they will not commit further criminal acts against society during the period of their incarceration. The basic difficulty, however, with the incapacitation argument is that we cannot or will not imprison a large enough percentage of the population to influence crime rates in this manner. It is likely that there will always be newcomers who are willing to take the risks and benefits associated with criminal behavior (Becker, 1968; Silberman, 1980). In fact, it appears from the data on recidivism among parolees that the prison experience is likely to result in more criminal activity following release from prison (Beck and Shipley, 1987). Thus, the rationale that crime will be prevented through the use of imprisonment appears legitimate only if we are willing to lock away all offenders (including the nonviolent) for life. Emotions might lead some to consider this possibility, but financial and ethical considerations make it infeasible. What are we left with, then? One of the most common alternatives in addressing the matter of increasing rates of imprisonment has been the development of the community corrections model. This is the topic for the next section.

The Community Corrections Model

In considering legal sanctions for those who are neither violent nor a threat to public safety, it is helpful to examine some of the more applied writings on how to minimize the use of imprisonment. If there is to be a significant reduction in the use of the prison sanction, it will be necessary to put forth a systematic community corrections ideology. It is acknowledged that one such model could be the constriction of criminal law and the criminal justice system in general. This approach has gained some acceptance in limited areas (e.g., victimless crimes and status offenses). But it is unlikely that decriminalization will be accepted for a broad enough range of offenses to dramatically reduce prison populations in a significant way. Therefore, it is mandatory that an intermediate model of crime control and correctional programming be specified—one that is based on sanctions that fall somewhere in between simple probation and imprisonment on the scale of punishment.

One such model that has evolved more formally in recent years has been the concept of "community corrections." While there has not been a thorough and systematic theory of community corrections put forth yet, the basic parameters of a noninstitutional, community approach to crime control have been outlined in some detail (e.g., Solomon, 1976; Fox, 1977; Smykla, 1981). Many of the programs suggested by the community corrections model have gained limited acceptance already—greater use of intensive probation, employment training, alternative education, youth shelters, drug-alcohol counseling centers, youth service bureaus, restitution programs, community service, volunteer programs, expanded social services, and so on. Yet the prison populations continue to increase.

The basic ideological problem is that these approaches are viewed as too lenient by many, and imprisonment is seen as the only "real" approach to dealing with crime. With the past dominance of the medical model in corrections, the common debate has been whether to punish or "treat" the real or imagined individual problems of offenders. Since, by definition, community approaches to crime control are supposed to go beyond just the individual pathology model to address broader social and economic problems, it is not surprising that such attempts have met with more than the usual amount of resistance. A community corrections approach to crime control is based on a broader view as to the causes of criminal behavior and a more refined concept of what constitutes appropriate correctional action.

The history of corrections has been one of combating the human penchant toward retaliation and punishment. Ironically, the development of the prison system was a response to the cruelty and degradation that characterized early societal reactions to crime. At present, it appears that community models of crime control are emerging simply as supplements to the prison systems rather than as alternatives. Prisons and community corrections need to be viewed in terms of a zero-sum game in order that community programs do not end up widening the scope of the criminal justice system. To follow the path of concurrent development is to negate the basic philosophy of community corrections as a less intrusive, less restrictive, and less costly *alternative* to imprisonment. The bottom line in assessing all community correctional programs has to be the degree to which the use of imprisonment is decreased.

Since the impetus provided by the newness of the community corrections concept has dissipated, it is now necessary for the movement to begin to recognize and systematically deal with the ideological obstacles. The basis of an alternative ideology of community corrections is a simple one: *nonviolent offenders can be dealt with most effectively and least expensively in a noninstitutional community setting where correctional personnel are familiar with the local community and social conditions.* To promulgate this ideology, it will be necessary to have strong voices advocating the philosophies of community corrections at all levels of government. Those in the traditional community correctional fields of probation, parole, and social work will need to join forces with those in the newer program areas to espouse a unified and systematic theory of community corrections. Professional associations can play an important role in this process by developing comprehensive theoretical frameworks and carrying out research which has specific implications for crime control policy. Individual practitioners and educators will also have to play more active roles in clarifying and supporting community approaches to dealing with nonviolent offenders, who constitute the majority of the prison populations. Official statistics show that only about 30% of all state and federal inmates were sentenced for the violent crimes of murder, rape, kidnapping, and assault (Innes, 1988).

In terms of political strategies, it is clear that the overall organization and structure of community corrections is highly important in generating effective political activity. Since community correctional programs are so widely dispersed and highly diverse, it is difficult to organize powerful local, state, and national associations capable of making strong statements to appropriate political units. Legislative mandates and formal administrative policies will be necessary to counterbalance the pronounced trends toward more repressive crime control policies. Following conviction, *disposition to noninstitutional community correctional alternatives must become a right rather than a privilege for the nonviolent offender.* To move in this direction, a great deal more thought will be required in spelling out the details of a community model of crime control, and much more activity will be necessary in presenting these concepts forcefully to policymakers and the public at large.

With continued increases in the numbers and lengths of prison sentences and the simultaneous concerns about governmental expenditures, some type of modification of the sentencing process seems inevitable. It is unlikely that this change will come about through the initiative of the legislative branch, as the passage of harsher criminal codes is the order of the day. Similarly, the ju-

diciary and legal profession have traditionally been less than en-
thusiastic about addressing the problems of prison overcrowding.
And given the vested interests of state departments of corrections,
it cannot be expected that these groups of correctional officials will
put forth energies to minimize the size of prison populations. The
strong forces pushing toward even greater overuse of imprisonment
will, as always, be difficult to counter. Along with the strategies
just discussed, it will be necessary to generate understandable research and data to respond to the arguments and rhetoric put forth
as justifications for the continued expansion of prison systems. The
following section will suggest some of the kinds of research that
will be needed along these lines and the types of data that will be
useful in formulating more reasoned imprisonment policies.

Research on the Use of Imprisonment

It is clear that any movement toward minimizing the use of
imprisonment will be accomplished only through advancements at
various levels. The ideological battle will require a certain degree
of empirical support. Overcoming the popular myths that are used
to justify our continued overuse of prisons will mean that a systematic data base must be generated. Specific concerns like prison
administrative procedures and inmate characteristics need to be
clarified by collecting simple descriptive information. It is difficult,
for instance, to collect even the most rudimentary statistics about
the granting of "good time" or the average length of time spent
for various offenses. Following a brief discussion of these applied
research issues, this section of the chapter will concentrate on
discussing some of the important theoretical research questions
about the use of imprisonment as a legal sanction.

Part of the problem in responding to calls for the expansion of
the prison network is the lack of access to important official data.
More than any other public organization, prisons have operated
"behind closed doors" making it impossible to cogently address
questionable claims. One particular such claim is that the prisons
are now dealing with the "hard core," since so many of the less
serious offenders are being diverted to community programs. This
rationale has been used to solicit more and more resources and to

justify the use of experimental programs where the most demeaning and repressive kinds of medical and behavioral research are undertaken. A number of relevant research questions demand attention. In what sense are the inmates supposedly "hard core"? Are they any more this way than in the past? Were they hard core when they entered prison? Will they be more hard core when they are returned to the community? What is the prognosis for the hard core? Most officials are quick to admit that they do not actually mean what the phrase "hard core" suggests to most people—violent and dangerous individuals. We need to be more honest and specific about just who does make up the prison population.

It is also difficult to gather information about the internal operating procedures of our prisons. The demands put forth by inmates during prison disturbances are generally related to basic administrative responsibilities. Typically the concerns of inmates center around issues like meals and food service, visitation privileges, opportunity for exercise, arbitrary and capricious punishments, random transfers to other institutions, absence of training programs, shortage of treatment personnel, denial of external communication, neglect of personal hygiene needs, and so on. While these are certainly straightforward and reasonable concerns, there is very rarely follow-up by anyone outside the prison system to monitor the promises made by officials during negotiations. It is important that concerned citizens, the media, and researchers be allowed to examine the problems that are constantly raised regarding prison management. While the above types of research may begin to help us to understand some of the immediate prison problems, long-range progress toward reducing the use of imprisonment will require more research on basic conceptual and ideological questions. Some suggestions have been put forth as to the important research topics that call for attention (e.g., Gilman, 1975). Precisely who is to be imprisoned? For what purposes? For how long? By whose decision? According to what criteria? For a fixed or indeterminate sentence? With or without good time and parole? It is this type of research agenda that gets to the core of the the imprisonment policies we now employ.

Another important ideological issue that has been largely ignored is the role of the media in shaping public perceptions about crime and imprisonment. Research in this area has suggested that the media plays a significant role in creating apparent "crime waves" (Fishman, 1978), and there is evidence that public perceptions about crime and criminal justice are more similar to the distorted portrayals by the media than to actual conditions (Greene and Bynum, 1982; Davis, 1952). With regard to the use of imprisonment, it is likely that the impact of media coverage contributes to a "lock 'em up" mentality, given the continual overemphasis on violent crime and sensationalism. It can be expected that support for more punitive crime control policies will grow if the media does not present a more balanced and less hysterical analysis of crime and society. Recent trends toward what has been called "tabloid television" have made this problem even worse. Shows like "Top Cops" and "Hard Copy," among numerous others, not only exploit the unfortunate tragedies that occur in society and play to our basest instincts, but they also gloss over the complex and sensitive dilemmas faced by the justice system.

Furthermore, it is important that researchers continue to examine cross-cultural differences in the way crime is defined and addressed. Writings with an international perspective serve as illuminating guideposts in assessing the current and proposed practices of the criminal justice system in the United States. The research discussed earlier in this chapter suggested that there are various ways of conceptualizing and operationalizing crime control policies. The underlying philosophies and operational procedures in comparable industrialized countries suggest that we have a great deal of room to explore the use of less drastic legal sanctions. Community corrections has been discussed in some detail, but there is not presently much enthusiasm for the concept. While some of the criticisms are indeed worth noting, it must be remembered that research on viable community approaches to crime control is crucial in combating the increasingly punitive trend.

In terms of direct impact, a most fruitful area for future research is the legislative process itself, as illustrated by McGarrell (1988) in his study of juvenile justice reform. Major criminal code revisions are being passed throughout the country, and our basic sentencing structure is shifting from a positivist-inspired indeterminacy model toward harsher fixed sentences. Several important questions remain unanswered about this phenomenon. Who has the most influence on crime control legislation? What types of data are considered in these deliberations? Are legislators presented with comprehensive proposals for less punitive criminal sanctions, and if so, why do they have such little impact? Is there any attempt to examine the implications and costs of new crime control legislation? How can legislation be secured that makes probation and other noninstitutional sanctions the preferred responses to most forms of nonviolent crime?

Finally, there are numerous pieces of specific legislation recently passed that call for closer scrutiny. These legal reforms are regularly discussed in the literature (e.g., National Council on Crime and Delinquency, 1975), but follow-up on the direct impact of policy changes is difficult to undertake and often shunned. Some particular issues include the mandatory sentence, habitual offender codes, stricter delinquency statutes, death penalty legislation, "crackdowns" on specific offenses, and mandated prison construction. It is also difficult to assess the impact of the occasional piece of innovative legislation restricting the scope of the legal process or lessening punishments. Decriminalization and decarceration have been accomplished in limited situations—some juvenile status offenses, various forms of gambling, private sexual acts between consenting adults, minor drug crimes, prostitution, abortion, and white-collar crime in industry and government. More intensive research is needed in these isolated instances of minimizing legal sanctions. They often go unnoticed and unexamined.

One last area of potentially useful research inside the prison walls is that of inmate governance. As Schwendinger and Schwendinger (1980) pointed out, the recognition of prisoners' rights in recent years will come to have meaning only when implemented and supported by organized inmate groups. Since court-mandated rights are sometimes manipulated and ignored even in the other phases of the criminal justice process, it is not surprising that rulings on the rights of inmates often have little impact in the closed prison environment. The most debilitating aspects of prison life result from the lawlessness and unfettered discretion in closed institutions. Research is sorely needed to demonstrate the necessity and desirability of inmate participation in prison governance.

The time may be coming when society is ready to question whether or not we can continue to afford what has been called "the extravagance of imprisonment" (Rector, 1975). Debate will continue to take place on ideological and political levels, but research activity will play a role in the eventual outcomes. Garofalo (1978) discussed the immediate and long-term benefits of diverse criminological research in the criminal justice system. Perhaps the most important result of intensive, critical research will be the attention focused on unworkable and unnecessary policies and practices. As it becomes clearer that imprisonment and overly punitive reactions to crime are counterproductive in many situations, the possibility for less restrictive community controls will increase. However, emotional reactions to crime based on sensationalism and fear can be attenuated only through sustained research efforts on a variety of fronts. Policies and laws based on sound research and accurate information will go a long way toward improving the overall effectiveness of the criminal justice system.

In chapter 2 we will take a closer look at the prison as it exists today. It has become more and more difficult over the last decade for researchers and journalists to gain access to prison systems, so one of our main sources of information about prison conditions now is the court document. This will be the primary source of information used in the next chapter to describe the nature of prison life following the population increases that have taken place over the last decade. It is unfortunate that there are so few other sources of data regarding prison conditions, but we can at least be grateful that litigation has been widespread during the population explosion that has overwhelmed corrections. Information from court documents provides an important window through which we may begin to observe the dimensions of the problems in prison systems of today.

2. U.S. Prisons in the Nineties

Sentencing Reform and Prisons

The rehabilitative ideal had gained increased prominence in our legal system throughout this century. Hopes had been high that by treating offenders we could prevent crime and alleviate social injustices. It was the indeterminate sentence that provided the legal mechanism through which the "medical model" was to be implemented. Correctional theories abounded, and there was an infusion of behavioral and social scientists in all facets of the justice system. Along with the traditional goals of incapacitation and retribution, the treatment ideal had come to be an important rationale of incarceration.

What follows is a discussion of the demise of the treatment model as accomplished through recent sentencing reforms. Attention will be focused on the implications of new presumptive sentencing codes for the management of prisons. Specifically, recent prison litigation will be reviewed to shed light on the conditions in prisons following the recent sentencing reforms. We will first review the prisoners' rights movement as it has evolved since the 1960s. Prison litigation based on Section 1983 of the U.S. Civil Rights Act will then be examined in order to better understand the acute overcrowding that has resulted from nationwide legislative activities in the reform of sentencing statutes. Also included in the chapter is a discussion of the impact of prison litigation and court involvement in the administration of prisons.

Since the establishment of the Walnut Street Jail in Philadelphia in 1794, the country has become more and more dependent on the use of imprisonment. Conceived originally as a humane alternative to brutal torture and public executions, prisons have a well-documented history of intractable problems. While we have become more willing (even eager) to use the prison sanction, we have been unable to make the prison experience an effective one. The failures of prisons are well documented (see, for example, Mathiesen, 1991). It has been argued that prisons are more criminogenic than preventive or rehabilitative, given the high rates of recidivism among former inmates. Nevertheless, the construction and use of prisons have continued unabated with no change in this trend visible for the near future. At least part of the reason for the increasing use of imprisonment is a major shift in sentencing philosophy that has taken place during the last decade.

The prison problem has been exacerbated by the national movement away from the rehabilitation concept and indeterminate sentencing. Impetus for this change came from the writings of a number of highly respected criminologists and legal scholars. One of the first proposals was the "justice model" as presented by Fogel in 1975. He proposed that flat, determinate sentencing would signal a shift toward more fair and uniform punishments that would in turn generate greater respect for the law and improve crime prevention. Others argued that the "just deserts" approach to sentencing would increase the deterrent value of penal sanctions and reemphasize the punishment philosophy of classical criminology (Van den Haag, 1974; Wilson, 1975; Dershowitz, 1976; Von Hirsch, 1977). Many of the ideas put forth for making punishments more clear and certain for each type of offense held potential for clarifying the sentencing decision. However, in the process of implementing these concepts, state legislatures tended to dilute the uniformity concept with resulting criminal codes that still involved much sentencing disparity (Goodstein et al., 1984). Most of the states passing new determinate or presumptive sentencing codes have increased the number of crimes punishable by imprisonment, as well as the amount of time spent in prisons for particular crimes, bringing about an overall increase in the level of commitments (Casper et al., 1983).

There have been a number of criticisms leveled at the "deserts" philosophy as explicated by the above authors. A major argument for the revision of indeterminate sentencing codes was the rejection of rehabilitation as a goal of corrections. Research and common knowledge had for years held that treatment programs in the prison did not work (there were some who argued that treatment had never seriously been undertaken). However, as Le Francois (1978) points out in his critique of the neoclassical view, there is a *blind faith in the effectiveness of deterrence* as a goal in sentencing even though the evidence on the validity of deterrence theory is as inconclusive as it was regarding rehabilitation (see Zimring and Hawkins, 1973). While there is good reason to question the use of imprisonment for rehabilitative purposes, the same type of skepticism is certainly warranted with respect to the deterrent value of incarceration. The indeterminate sentencing model had also been characterized as too lenient although, as we saw in the last chapter, the lengths of criminal sentences and incarceration rates in the United States have been as harsh as those of any nation in the world, with the possible exceptions of those repressive countries that blatantly imprison for political reasons.

Another major criticism of the indeterminate model of sentencing was the disparity of sentences. The notion of "fair and equal" punishments was central to many of the writings on presumptive sentencing. It is questionable whether disparity has now been reduced. It appears that sentencing reforms have only shifted discretion and the responsibility for disparity from parole boards and correctional personnel to judges and prosecutors (Lagoy et al., 1978). There is little reason to believe that judges and prosecutors will use their broadened discretionary powers any more consistently than correctional experts to achieve equity in sentencing. Also, the elimination of parole has led to the increased use of good time laws as a management tool to control behavior and maintain discipline inside the walls. This only serves to locate responsibility for time served in the hands of the least qualified custodial staff and make discretion even less open to review. Relatedly, it has also been found that inmates develop a more negative attitude toward custodial staff (Davies, 1985), which is not surprising since this group must now directly lengthen sentence times through disciplinary writeups. While the decisions of parole boards were always problematic, they were at least more open to scrutiny than the internal decisions made by disciplinary committees.

Perhaps the most scathing criticism of the just deserts model is Braithwaite's (1982) charge that harsher sentences inevitably apply just deserts more stringently to the poor convicted of street crimes and less stringently to other groups such as white-collar offenders.

He argues that because of the inevitable practice of selective enforcement and the unequal application of sanctions, a just deserts model only serves to exaggerate the differential handling of the rich and the poor. The literature is replete with evidence demonstrating the importance of extralegal factors such as race and socioeconomic status in the disposition of criminal cases (e.g., Atkins and Pogrebin, 1978; Reiss, 1974; Mann, 1989). It can only be expected that these patterns will become more pronounced as the harshness of sentences increases.

Perhaps the most immediate problem with the deserts philosophy as it has been implemented thus far is the unmanageable increases in prison populations that have resulted. With the exception of the state of Minnesota, there has been little consideration of the realities of sentencing reform as it relates to prison capacities in the departments of corrections (Knapp, 1984). The U.S. Department of Justice (1989) reports that much of the surge in prison populations can be attributed to the passage of determinate and presumptive sentencing codes beginning in 1975. Populations in state prisons increased not only in numbers, but in the proportion of long-term prisoners as well. The Justice Department reports have noted regularly over the last several years that imprisonment rates continue to reach new all-time highs. Furthermore, the research by Cahalan (1979) reminds us again that imprisonment rates would be much higher if juveniles and those serving sentences in local jails were included. What makes this data on prison population so perplexing is that the dramatic increases have taken place during a period when crime rates have not been soaring. As Doleschal (1979) notes in discussing the victimization studies carried out by the U.S. Census Bureau, crime rates have remained "remarkably stable" since 1973. Even using more recent data from the FBI (1989), it is clear that the increases in crime over the past decade do not begin to correspond to the increases in imprisonment rates. In addition, there has been a proliferation of community correctional programs during this time aimed at diverting nonviolent offenders out of prison systems. The numbers of offenders in all types of old and new community programs have increased, with the commonly heard rationale being that such programs are alleviating the prison overcrowding problem.

Common assumptions about the effects of imprisonment on crime rates are simplistic and unproven. Sentencing and imprisonment rates seem to be more a function of citizens' perceptions, political rhetoric, and the "evidence" from officials of the justice system (particularly the police, prosecutors, and prison officials). Generally, criminal justice officials and legislators claim that they are merely responding to demands of the citizenry for harsher punishments, as if they themselves played no role in shaping public opinion. However, Giari (1979) argues that these groups create the public demand and manipulate public opinion. Perhaps the best example of this phenomenon is the distortion of the nature of the prison population. Giari notes that politicians and officials commonly reject early release programs and alternatives to prison because of the supposed threat to public safety. Rarely mentioned by officials and ignored by the media is the fact that a large proportion of the inmate population is made up of the nonviolent property offender who will "be back on the street" soon anyway. Correctional officials admit privately that a large percentage (from 50% to 75%) of all inmates could likely be released without endangering the safety of citizens.

The basic problem with the presumptive sentencing movement has been that legislatures have used it as a political tool to justify haphazard "get tough" criminal code revisions. Prior to the widespread adoption of sentencing reforms, there were predictions as to the impact of such changes. One study concluded that sentences under a new presumptive code would increase approximately 50% overall for first offenders and as much as 120% for the offense of burglary (Clear et al., 1978). Brewer, Beckett, and Holt (1981) estimated that the overall number of commitments would also increase drastically. The combination of more commitments and longer sentences is beginning to have a staggering effect on incarceration rates and prison management. There has been a basic organizational contradiction in that the harsher code revisions led to *large increases in prison populations without corresponding increases in funding* that would allow correctional officials to deal effectively with the added responsibilities (Greenberg and Humphries, 1980). It is this double problem of overcrowding and underfunding that has brought about a rash of prison litigation. Before examining the 1983 suits that illustrate the extent of problems in prisons today, it will be useful to review the development of prisoners' rights and prison litigation since the 1960s.

The Prisoners' Rights Movement

Beginning in the early part of the 1960s, the courts began to take a somewhat different stance toward the matter of prisoners' rights. The earlier notions of "civil death" and "slaves of the state" were taken to mean that upon conviction and sentencing to a term of imprisonment, the inmate lost all rights and was under the absolute control of correctional authorities. Courts had traditionally followed what was termed the "hands off" doctrine. Based on the historical concept of separation of powers, the courts showed deference to the legislatures and the departments of corrections in the executive branch. Legislators would determine prison conditions through funding levels, but prison administration was considered to be a technical matter that was best left to those who knew and understood the prisons from an administrative perspective.

The National Advisory Commission (1973) outlined the four basic areas of legal action in the prisoners' rights movement. These include (1) the right to access to the courts and (2) First Amendment rights, as well as (3) rights related to the conditions of confinement and (4) the procedural practices of prison officials. While it is important to understand the role of the courts in prison matters over the last three decades, a note of caution should be raised at this point. Indeed, the courts have come to play a role in the exasperating field of prison administration. The Supreme Court and federal appellate courts have heard hundreds of cases in recent years dealing with nearly every aspect of prison life and prison management. Judges have often ruled in favor of the inmate positions and have written far-reaching decisions that have accurately portrayed the harsh realities of prison life. Yet we should not be misled into thinking that the court decisions of the '60s, '70s and '80s have significantly improved the way prisons operate; one writer has sardonically referred to the "impotence of correctional law" (Thomas, 1980).

While court decisions have been effective in certain limited areas like the banning of corporal punishments, judicial mandates have often been ignored and circumvented when they address major issues in prison administration. Furthermore, the courts have now again become hesitant to intervene in prison affairs under the Rehnquist court. Except in rare instances where court monitors have been appointed, states and correctional officials have found numerous methods for avoiding the orders handed down by the courts. Sometimes the court rulings are simply disregarded. The closed nature of prisons makes it difficult, if not impossible, to observe the internal mechanisms of prison management. It has also been common for officials to plead lack of funds. In many instances, correctional officials have actually been pleased with the court rulings against their departments, in the hopes of finally receiving the funding necessary to operate in a more competent manner. Legislatures have been less than willing to appropriate funding to comply with court orders, and legislators have been outspoken in their criticisms of the courts. It should not be surprising, then, that prison conditions today are not much different from what they were prior to the prisoners' rights movement. This movement, however, has still been consequential in that the courts have made it clear that prisoners can no longer be considered "slaves of the state" and overtly treated in ways that are capricious and degrading to human dignity. Some examples follow.

The Supreme Court first recognized a limited right to access to the courts in *Ex Parte Hull* (1941). This decision was notable primarily in a theoretical sense because there was almost no litigation dealing with prisoners' rights for the next several years. Access to the courts was addressed in a more practical sense by the U.S. Supreme Court in *Johnson v. Avery* (1969). In this landmark decision, the High Court dealt with the issue of whether "jailhouse lawyers" could assist other inmates (particularly the illiterate) in preparing habeas corpus petitions that challenged the legality of their incarceration. This decision granted inmates the right to provide assistance to fellow prisoners if the prison did not offer alternatives for inmates seeking postconviction relief. Writ writers had long been a nuisance and an embarrassment to prison officials. Usually long-term inmates, these jailhouse lawyers were very knowledgeable about the law and had successes in raising issues in the courts that had to do with prison procedures and conditions. It was understandable from a management perspective that prison authorities would discipline writ writers and make it difficult for them to provide this valuable service. The Court reasoned in the Johnson case that assistance must be provided since, otherwise, valid constitutional claims could not possibly be heard.

Beginning in the early 1960s, the appellate courts began to demonstrate a willingness to hear specific complaints of prisoners. As might be expected, the earliest pronouncements of the courts on prison matters had to do with First Amendment guarantees of freedom of religion, clearly one of the most cherished rights in our Constitution. The question of religious discrimination was addressed by the U.S. District of Columbia Court in *Fulwood v. Clemmer* (1962). This decision recognized the Black Muslim faith as a religion and acknowledged the right of Muslim inmates to practice the religion of their choice unless prison officials could demonstrate that such activities would pose a threat to institutional security. The Supreme Court further recognized the First Amendment's protection from religious discrimination in *Cruz v. Beto* (1972), wherein the rights of Buddhist prisoners to observe their religion in a manner comparable to that of other religious groups were mandated.

Other First Amendment issues were heard by the courts that illustrated the changing relationship between prisons and the judiciary. With regard to another of our most cherished rights, the courts have recognized in a limited way the freedom of speech inside the prison walls. For example, the *Nolan v. Fitzpatrick* (1971) decision recognized the right of prisoners to communicate with newspapers unless their letters contained contraband or other objectionable material. And the Supreme Court found the blanket censorship of all inmate mail to be unconstitutional in *Procunier v. Martinez* (1974). Noting the importance of inmate communications with their attorneys and court officials, this ruling concluded that censorship of mail was acceptable only if there was a "substantial governmental interest" such as maintenance of order and security within the institution. In addition to the First Amendment rulings, the courts also began to hear cases dealing with substantive rights under the Eighth Amendment and procedural issues based on the due process guarantees of the Fifth and Fourteenth Amendments.

The "cruel and unusual punishment" clause of the Eighth Amendment has been the basis of numerous prisoners' rights suits challenging various disciplinary practices of prison officials. Although the courts have shown restraint in applying the Eighth Amendment strictures to prisons, there have been certain instances where the use of punishment methods have been found to be unconstitutional. For example, in *Jordan v. Fitzharris* (1966), it was ruled that placement in the strip cells at Soledad Prison was to be terminated because of the deplorable conditions, including severe heat and cold and a hole in the ground for a toilet. Relatedly, the Supreme Court concluded that placement in solitary confinement in the Arkansas segregation cells for longer than thirty days was in violation of the Eighth Amendment (*Hutto v. Finney*, 1978). The use of whippings and most other forms of corporal punishment have also been found to be unconstitutional under the Eighth Amendment through the *Jackson v. Bishop* (1968) decision.

Some of the most far-reaching court decisions in terms of the Eighth Amendment have been those dealing with prison medical practices. As one of the most important conditions of confinement, given the violence in prisons, the availability of medical care is a pressing issue inside the walls. The *Newman v. Alabama* (1972) case was the first in which the court decided that the medical care in an entire state prison system was constitutionally unacceptable. As a result of dire shortages of physicians and nurses, reliance on untrained inmates as paramedics, and the intentional failures to treat the sick and injured, the court ruled that medical care did not meet even the barest minimal standards. The Supreme Court addressed the same issue in *Estelle v. Gamble* (1976) and created what has stood as the basic standard for evaluating the medical care received by inmates. It must be shown that there is "deliberate indifference" to the serious medical needs of prisoners in order to successfully challenge the medical services in prison. Of course, this guideline has made it very difficult to direct further attention to the medical care provided by prison authorities. It is difficult to show that prison staff are deliberately indifferent.

The basis for the 1983 suit to be discussed in the next section was formulated in *Holt v. Sarver* (1970). This landmark decision dealt with the overall conditions of confinement within the Arkansas prison system. That system had generally been known as one of the worst correctional systems in the nation, and there was protracted testimony regarding nearly every aspect of prison operations. The unique feature of the *Holt* decision was the finding that *the "totality of conditions" was so deplorable that confinement in such institutions, in and of itself, constituted cruel and unusual punishment.* This line of thinking came to form the essence of the rulings handed down in many 1983 suits. There was a shift by the courts away from considering single issues in the prison setting toward a more encompassing view that took into account the nature of the total prison environment.

A final comment should be made with respect to the procedural rights of prisoners. The due process clauses of the Fifth and Fourteenth became important in the prisoners' rights movement as the courts began to recognize the importance of disciplinary procedures as used by correctional officials. Table 2.1 presents a summary of some of the most important Supreme Court cases that have clarified the procedural rights of inmates at various stages of the correctional process. In terms of prison operations, *Wolff v. McDonnell* (1974) defined the due process requirements for inmate disciplinary proceedings that involve the most serious kinds of punishments (i.e., loss of good time and solitary confinement). It is clear that constitutional safeguards for prisoners are somewhat less stringent than those for defendants who are accused of a crime. Most importantly, there is a very limited right to counsel at the various decision-making points in the correctional system. While there are rights to be given a notice of charges and to have the opportunity to be heard in person, there are only limited rights to confront and cross-examine witnesses and to present evidence on one's behalf. This series of decisions has laid some parameters for the practices of correctional officials, although they still maintain a high degree of discretion in deciding how to deal with inmates and internal prison problems.

As we will see in the following section, the sometimes arbitrary and capricious use of discretion is one of the major complaints that arises in the prison litigation suits of today. The particular case discussed below is but one of many 1983 suits that challenge conditions of confinement in prisons across the United States. It is presented as an example, since the nature of class action suits has been comparable around the nation during the last decade. The

Table 2.1. Due Process Rights of Inmates at Various Hearing Stages, as Determined by the Supreme Court, 1972–1979

Parole Revocation Hearing (*Morrisey v. Brewer*, 1972)	Probation Revocation Hearing (*Gagnon v. Scarpelli*, 1973)	Prison Disciplinary Hearing Where Punishment Is Loss of Goodtime Credit or Solitary Confinement (*Wolff v. McDonnell*, 1974)	Classification (Disciplinary) Hearing Where Inmate is Subject to Involuntary Transfer to a Less Desirable Institution (*Meachum v. Fano*, 1976)	Parole Grant Hearing (*Greenholtz v. Inmates of Nebraska Penal Complex*, 1979)
Written notice of alleged violation of conditions of parole	Written notice of alleged violations of conditions of probation	Written notice of charge at least 24 hours before hearing	No rights under the due process clause; transfers do not jeopardize any vested "liberty interest" and entirely within the discretionary realm of prison officials	Due Process Clause of Fourteenth Amendment does not cover inmates at the parole grant hearing stage. Specifically, inmates being considered for parole have no right to counsel, to present documentary evidence in their behalf, or to a statement of the "particular evidence" parole board relied on in denying parole
Hearing before a neutral and detached body, such as a parole board, whose members need not include lawyers	Hearing before a neutral and detached body	Hearing before an impartial tribunal or fact-finder		

Table 2.1.—Continued

Parole Revocation Hearing (*Morrisey v. Brewer*, 1972)	Probation Revocation Hearing (*Gagnon v. Scarpelli*, 1973)	Prison Disciplinary Hearing Where Punishment Is Loss of Goodtime Credit or Solitary Confinement (*Wolff v. McDonnell*, 1974)	Classification (Disciplinary) Hearing Where Inmate is Subject to Involuntary Transfer to a Less Desirable Institution (*Meachum v. Fano*, 1976)	Parole Grant Hearing (*Greenholtz v. Inmates of Nebraska Penal Complex*, 1979)
No right to counsel	Limited right for indigent probationers and parolees to appointed counsel, to be determined on a case-by-case basis; grounds for refusing to grant request for counsel to be stated in the record	No right to counsel; but in unusually complex cases and those involving illiterate inmates, the accused should be allowed to seek aid from a fellow inmate or be given assistance from the staff		
Opportunity to be heard in person	Opportunity to be heard in person	Opportunity to be heard in person and to present defense		
Limited "right" to confront and cross-examine witnesses, unless hearing officer finds good cause for not allowing cross-examination; in effect, no right to confrontation and cross-examination	Limited "right" to confront and cross-examine witnesses, unless hearing officer finds good cause for not allowing cross-examination; in effect, no right to confrontation and cross-examination	No right to confront and cross-examine witnesses		

Opportunity to present witnesses and documentary evidence	Opportunity to present witnesses and documentary evidence	Recommendation (no right) that inmate be allowed to call witnesses and to present documentary evidence when doing so would not be unduly hazardous to institutional safety or correctional goals, according to the discretion of the disciplinary committee
Disclosure to parolee of evidence used against him/her	Disclosure to probationer of evidence used against him/her	
Written statement of evidence relied on and reasons for revoking parole	Written statement of evidence relied on and reasons for revoking probation	Written statement by fact-finder regarding evidence and reasons for disciplinary action; the statement need not be a full transcript of the hearing, and it may exclude evidence where necessary to maintain personal safety or institutional security.

Source: Gerald D. Robin, *Introduction to the Criminal Justice System* (3rd Ed.). New York: Harper and Row Publishers, 1987.

issues and concerns raised in this case reflect the kinds of problems that have been exposed in most of our state prison systems.

Prison Conditions Today

Issues before the Courts

As the prisoners' rights movement was crisis driven, it is not surprising that the extent of prison litigation has mushroomed in recent years. At least thirty states have now been under court order to improve prison conditions (Gaes and McGuire, 1985). The two primary tests of cruel and unusual punishment have been practices that "shock the general conscience" and punishments that are unnecessary because "less restrictive means" would serve the state interest as well (Kerper and Kerper, 1974). The 1983 suit has become the most appropriate instrument for addressing prison problems, since class action filings are permitted and broad injunctive relief may be sought through revised regulations, court monitoring, and/or master plans.

French v. Owens (1985) was a class action suit brought on behalf of all inmates at the Indiana Reformatory. This case is representative of recent 1983 suits and illustrates the broad range of problems faced by prison administrators with prisons in crisis. The Reformatory is a maximum security facility built in 1923. The population in August, 1978, at the beginning of the suit and just prior to the implementation of a new presumptive sentencing code, was 1,215. By the time the decision was handed seven years later, the population had increased over 60% to a record level of 1,972. The major complaints raised in the suit were the following: overcrowding, poor living conditions, inadequate medical care, lack of safety and security, unhealthy food services, inadequate educational and vocational programs, an arbitrary system of prison discipline, and insufficient access to the courts. In its ruling, the court referred to the general principles set forth in *Robinson v. California* (1962), making the prohibition of cruel and unusual punishment applicable to the states through the Fourteenth Amendment, as well as *Estelle v. Gamble* (1976), which stated that prison confinement is subject to the strictures of the Eighth Amendment. Also quoted was *Trop v. Dulles* (1957), wherein punishment was to be made compatible with "evolving standards of decency that mark the progress of a maturing society."

Prior to discussing the findings and order of the court in the *French* case, it is instructive to remember the continued reservations of the judiciary to intervene in prison affairs. The court in this case clearly acknowledged that incarceration must involve the withdrawal of some rights and privileges. It also recognized the complex and contradictory goals of prisons, as well as the need to carefully weigh the relationship between rehabilitation and security. In the conclusion of the Memorandum of Decision in *French* this position was stated more pointedly:

> Certainly this court has no objection to requiring lawbreakers to serve terms of imprisonment, and neither does it believe that a prison should be a country club. However, when a prison has been found to be operated in plain violation of the law, the Court has the power, and it is its duty, to order appropriate remedial action.

Findings of Fact

A brief review of the findings of fact in the *French* case will make clear the myriad problems faced by correctional administrators today. As with most of the old maximum-security prisons which make up the backbone of our nation's prison system, the physical plant at the Indiana Reformatory is beyond repair. The court found that living quarters do not have adequate ventilation systems, since the grates at the back of each cell are uncleaned and clogged with dirt and lint. Many of the devices for opening and closing windows are defective so the windows are sealed shut. The hot and cold air systems are found to be inadequate, resulting in cells being too hot in the summer and too cold in the winter. In-cell lighting is generally insufficient, and outside windows are so dirty that the amount of natural light is diminished. Toilet stools and sinks in the cells are scabrous according to the court, and facilities are literally uncleanable because of age and deterioration. Many shower areas contain an accumulation of grime and many have a noticeable mold growth. The physical conditions are generally worse in the segregation units.

With respect to exercise and recreation, the prison was found to be in repeated violation of its own state laws. Some inmates are held in their cells for twenty-four hours every day except for a shower, and many inmates spend in excess of twenty-two hours daily in their cells. The court's findings also indicated that state laws regarding medical and mental health services for inmates are routinely violated. Most medical services are delivered by "technicians" presumably under the supervision of the prison's one doctor. The record is replete with evidence of inadequate medical care, which has often resulted in personal harm. Inmates have gone for months without detection of communicable tuberculosis. It is estimated that 8%–12% of the inmates are acutely or severely psychotic, but the psychologists on duty cannot prescribe medication and have an antimedical bias. This has resulted in psychotic inmates being chained to a bed with all four limbs completely restrained in a spread-eagle fashion as "treatment" when they act out their delusions. Expert witnesses called by both sides characterized this practice as "medieval."

The Reformatory was also found to be in violation of state laws regarding minimal provision of educational and vocational programs. A total of 260 inmates were involved in education programs and 136 in vocational training. This was less than 20% of the inmate population. In practical terms, participation in educational programs is discouraged, since those attending school receive the lowest inmate pay rate at forty cents per hour. Inmates under protective custody and in administrative segregation are not permitted to make use of the library nor educational programs and are thus excluded completely from any type of meaningful intellectual activity. Another 45% of the inmate population hold institutional jobs or are involved in prison industries, although many of these positions entail only two or three hours of work each day. The remaining 35% of the population are not assigned to any type of activity on a regular basis. Over one-third of the population then finds itself in the state of "enforced idleness," which is probably the most debilitating and self-defeating situation to endure while serving a prison term.

In terms of the general environment, the court found the institution to be in clear violation of numerous fire, sanitation, and public health laws. The last report by the state fire marshall listed

122 separate remedial activities required to place buildings in compliance with state fire laws. Recent inspections of the kitchen and commissary found there to be mice and roaches. The kitchen floor is literally uncleanable because of holes and cracks, some of the ceiling is missing, and many of the walls are cracked. Live cockroaches and fresh mice droppings were observable in the storeroom. In the dining room, food-warming tables are inoperative and hot foods are served below safe temperatures. In the cellblocks, birds and flying insects enter through unscreened windows, and poor plumbing allows the multiplication of rodents and other vermin. Given the absence of adequate ventilation systems, conditions exist which are conducive to the spread of various communicable diseases.

It is within this scenario that the court addressed the primary issues in the suit—overcrowding and double celling. There was much testimony from inmates, corrections officials, and expert witnesses for both sides regarding the impact of overcrowding and understaffing on levels of hostility and violence. The findings of fact indicate that severe forms of violence, including stabbings, bludgeonings, and homosexual rapes, occur with distressing frequency. Severe injuries and fatalities have resulted from these incidents. Lesser forms of violence such as harassment, threats, intimidation, strikings, and beatings were found to be routine. In noting the change that took place when double celling began, one employee testified that tension in the cellblocks had increased 100% to a "blowing level," sanitation had gone downhill, and much more arguing and fighting had begun to take place. These types of problems have always been present to some degree in maximum-security prisons. However, current conditions create an atmosphere in which staff and inmates alike fear for their lives on a minute-to-minute basis, losing all respect for other human beings. The state has been grossly negligent in upholding its legal commitments to provide for the physical safety of those sentenced to state institutions (not to mention those who are employed by the state).

In the *French* case, the Department of Corrections argued that double celling does not constitute cruel and unusual punishment, citing the *Bell v. Wolfish* (1979) and *Rhodes v. Chapman* (1981) decisions handed down by the U.S. Supreme Court. These cases, however, emanated from the Metropolitan Correctional Center in

New York City and the Southern Ohio Correctional Facility, respectively. The Indiana Reformatory is a stark contrast to these new, clean, and relatively safe institutions. In its consideration of the claims in this case, the court again emphasized the importance of the notion of totality of conditions. It cited *Gates v. Collier* (1974) in defining the principle of totality as it relates to prison conditions: "Each factor separately . . . may not rise to constitutional dimensions; however, the totality of these circumstances is the infliction of punishment on inmates violative of the Eighth Amendment." Accordingly, the court found that overcrowding at the Reformatory, coupled with all of the other conditions, considered as a whole, constituted cruel and inhumane treatment of inmates in violation of the Eighth and Fourteenth Amendments.

While the court found the defendants, in their official capacities, to be in violation of both state and federal laws, it clearly put the blame on the elected legislators of the state. The court further noted that General Assemblies through the years have continually lengthened sentences for violations of criminal laws while failing to appropriate even minimally sufficient funds for the normal upkeep of penal institutions. Legislatures had also failed to appropriate adequate funds to hire qualified personnel and to establish programs mandated by state law even before the present crisis. Overall, the situation is one in which there is little or no coordination between the judicial branch, which does the sentencing, the executive branch, which must administer the prisons, and the legislative branch, which prescribes punishment levels *and* is responsible for providing operational funding.

It has been reasonably argued that the legislatures, being the most democratically representative branch of government, should maintain the power to set criminal punishments. However, when legislatures are negligent in their funding capacity to the extent that punishment cannot be administered within the bounds of evolving standards of decency, it is the role of the appellate courts in our system of checks and balances to address this abrogation of legislative responsibility. The 1983 suit appears to be the primary tool for pushing this issue during the current national crisis of prison overcrowding. Prisons remain the most hidden and demeaning institutions in our society. The 1983 suit is a first step toward exposing prison conditions to public scrutiny and dispelling myths about prisons being "country clubs." Of equal importance, the suits are beginning to force legislators to acknowledge that "get tough" rhetoric often results in expensive practices that threaten the liquidity of already strained state budgets.

In a civilized society, punishment by imprisonment is costly. Table 2.2 indicates the magnitude of the problems we faced in corrections nearly ten years ago. And the situation has gone downhill since that time! There has been much disagreement as to the most appropriate and feasible responses to the 1983 suit. In the section that follows, we will look at some of the various responses that have followed court rulings with an eye toward the potential implications of the increasing involvement of judges in the management of prisons.

Responses to 1983 Suits

Continued Expansion

The successful prison class action suit generates a host of reactions from corrections officials and legislators. There is some positive reaction such as proposing early release programs and sentencing alternatives for the nonviolent offender. For the most part, however, the reactions are not realistic in terms of the problems, and they have been designed to avoid the basic incongruity between the number of sentenced offenders and availability of resources. As a result of such cases, the courts tend to order major steps to be taken in hiring more personnel, upgrading prison programs, and repairing the physical facilities. These steps would require large outlays of scarce tax money. Most importantly, the courts often order an end to double celling and a reduction of population to comply with the rated capacity level of the institution.

Given the amount of funding required to address the required changes from 1983 suits, it would seem most practical to begin addressing the population issue by seeking alternatives for the nonviolent offenders. Besides increasing commitments and sentence lengths, presumptive sentencing codes have further exacerbated the prison problem by eliminating the traditional safety valve within an indeterminate sentencing model. The parole process, with all

Table 2.2.   Pending Litigation

A report on prison conditions, released in December 1983 by the National Prison Project of the American Civil Liberties Union (ACLU), shows the following legal activity for the respective States. The report includes court decrees or pending litigation, involving the entire State prison system or the major institutions in the State that deal with overcrowding and / or the total conditions of confinement. It does not include jails except for the District of Columbia.

1. Alabama: The entire State prison system is under court order dealing with total conditions and overcrowding. To relieve overcrowding and back-up of State prisoners in county jails, 400 State prisoners (number later modified) were ordered released. A second prisoner release order was issued; a stay was granted; the order was thereafter vacated. The district court entered an order establishing a four-person committee to monitor compliance with previous orders. A further release order was entered by the district court in November 1983, and applications for a stay were denied by the Court of Appeals and the Supreme Court.

2. Arizona: The State penitentiary is being operated under a series of court orders and consent decrees dealing with overcrowding, classification, and other conditions.

3. California: The State penitentiary at San Quentin is under court order on overcrowding and conditions. Order includes requirement that a special master be appointed.

4. Colorado: The State maximum security penitentiary is under court order on total conditions and overcrowding. The prison was declared unconstitutional and ordered to be ultimately closed.

5. Connecticut: The Hartford Correctional Center operated by the State is under court order dealing with overcrowding and some conditions.

6. Delaware: The State penitentiary is under court order dealing primarily with overcrowding and some conditions.

7. Florida: The entire State prison system is under court order dealing with overcrowding. A settlement on overcrowding has been approved.

8. Georgia: The State penitentiary at Reidsville is under court order on total conditions and overcrowding. A special master was appointed in June 1979.

9. Hawaii: The State penitentiary in Honolulu is being challenged in a totality of conditions suit.

10. Idaho: The women's prison is being challenged on total conditions.

11. Illinois: The State penitentiary at Menard is under court order on total conditions and overcrowding. The State penitentiary at Pontiac was under a court order enjoining double-celling and dealing with overcrowding. Litigation is pending at other institutions.

12. Indiana: The State prison at Pendleton was found unconstitutional on total conditions and overcrowding. The State penitentiary at Michigan City is under a court order on overcrowding and other conditions.

13. Iowa: The State penitentiary is under court order on overcrowding and a variety of other conditions.

14. Kansas: The State penitentiary is under a consent decree on total conditions.

15. Kentucky: The State penitentiary and reformatory are under court order by virtue of a consent decree on overcrowding and some conditions. The women's State prison is under court order on a variety of conditions.

16. Louisiana: The State penitentiary is under court order dealing with overcrowding and a variety of conditions.

17. Maine: The State penitentiary was challenged on overcrowding and a variety

of conditions. The trial court granted relief only as to restraint cells and otherwise dismissed the complaint, appeal pending.

18. Maryland: The two State penitentiaries were declared unconstitutional on overcrowding.

19. Massachusetts: The maximum security unit at the State prison in Walpole is being challenged on total conditions. A decision for the prison officials was affirmed in part and reversed in part and remanded.

20. Michigan: The women's prison is under court order. The entire men's prison system is under court order on overcrowding, and the State prison at Jackson is being challenged on other conditions.

21. Mississippi: The entire State prison system is under court order dealing with overcrowding and total conditions.

22. Missouri: The State penitentiary is under court order on overcrowding and some conditions.

23. Nevada: The State penitentiary is under court order on overcrowding and total conditions. New addition to State penitentiary under court order on total conditions.

24. New Hampshire: The State penitentiary is under court order dealing with total conditions and overcrowding.

25. New Mexico: The State penitentiary is under court order on overcrowding and total conditions. A special master was appointed in June 1983.

26. North Carolina: A lawsuit was filed in 1978 at Central Prison in Raleigh on overcrowding and conditions and a similar lawsuit is pending involving the women's prison.

27. Ohio: The State prison at Lucasville was under court order on overcrowding. The State prison at Columbus was under court order resulting from a consent decree on total conditions and overcrowding and was required to be closed in 1983, actually closing in September 1984. The State prison at Mansfield is being challenged on total conditions.

28. Oklahoma: The State penitentiary is under court order on total conditions, and the entire State prison system is under court order on overcrowding. The district court's decision to retain jurisdiction to insure continued compliance was upheld.

29. Oregon: The State penitentiary was under court order on overcrowding. Appeal pending; stay granted. On remand, the district court determined there was no 8th amendment violation.

30. Pennsylvania: The women's prison is being challenged on conditions and practices.

31. Rhode Island: The entire State system is under court order on overcrowding and total conditions. A special master was appointed in September 1977.

32. South Carolina: The State penitentiary is being challenged on overcrowding and conditions. The entire prison system is being challenged on overcrowding and conditions.

33. South Dakota: The State penitentiary at Sioux Falls is being challenged on a variety of conditions.

34. Tennessee: The entire State prison system declared unconstitutional on total conditions. Decision in August 1978 with preliminary order closing one unit by State court judge. The entire system was held unconstitutional in the Federal court. Population order reduced and a special master appointed.

35. Texas: The entire State prison system has been declared unconstitutional on

Table 2.2.—Continued

overcrowding and conditions. A special master was appointed. On appeal, the district court order was *affirmed in part, vacated in part,* and *vacated without prejudice* in part for further hearings.

36. Utah: The State penitentiary is being operated under a consent decree on overcrowding and some conditions.
37. Vermont: State prison closed.
38. Virginia: The State prison at Powhatan is under a consent decree dealing with overcrowding and conditions. The maximum security prison at Mecklenburg is under court order dealing with various practices and conditions. The State penitentiary at Richmond is being challenged on the totality of conditions. Trial court decision dismissed the complaint. Appeal pending.
39. Washington: The State reformatory is being challenged on overcrowding and conditions. The State penitentiary at Walla Walla has been declared unconstitutional on overcrowding and conditions. A special master has been appointed.
40. West Virginia: The State penitentiary at Moundsville is under court order on overcrowding and conditions.
41. Wisconsin: The State prison at Waupun is being challenged on overcrowding.
42. Wyoming: The State penitentiary is being operated under terms of a stipulation and consent decree. The Federal court relinquished jurisdiction in early 1983.
43. District of Columbia: The District jails are under court order on overcrowding and conditions. On remand, court ordered limit on period of double-celling and increase in staff. New trial held on overcrowding and conditions in November 1983. District Prison at Lorton is under a court order on overcrowding and conditions.
44. Puerto Rico: The Commonwealth Penitentiary is under court order on overcrowding and conditions. The entire commonwealth prison system is under court order dealing with overcrowding and conditions.
45. Virgin Islands: Territorial prison is under court order dealing with conditions and overcrowding.

Source: Eileen Garry. *Options to Reduce Prison Crowding.* Washington, D.C.: National Institute of Justice, 1984. Appendix A, p. 21.

its problems, did allow correctional officials a certain measure of control over inmate behavior and release time. Under the current codes, it will require specific legislation to alter prison population trends (e.g., "caps" legislation setting population limits). As far as the departments of corrections are concerned, they have learned that the "loss" of a major suit can indeed mean much more money, as Collins (1986) has pointed out. However, the funding provided for the expansionist policies is never sufficient to keep pace with the continual increases in numbers of inmates.

Most of the proposals put forth legislatively with regard to the 1983 rulings involve more of the same ineffective, expensive, and destructive approaches. The first reaction to most similar court orders is to appeal in hopes of ignoring the entire matter. Bills will likely be introduced to appropriate massive amounts of funding for the construction of new prisons and dormitory additions to the present facilities. This takes place at a time when there are significant decreases in the size of the crime-prone population and when crime rates are remaining at relatively stable levels. Another popular reaction among the states has been the conversion of old mental hospitals and other dilapidated institutions to correctional facilities, or even the creation of fenced "tent cities" such as in Texas. Relatedly, there has been legislation requiring that short-term inmates serve their sentences in already overcrowded and inadequate county jails. Funds for work-release centers and other "brick and mortar" projects have often been available, although the notion of work-release has recently fallen into disfavor. The single-minded approach to solving prison overcrowding through expansion and construction is rationalized with rhetoric about protecting society from violent criminals. But in Indiana, as an example, the Department of Correction's own statistics indicate that approximately 80% of the inmates sentenced annually are non-violent property offenders.

Depopulation

The alternative to continued expansion of the prison system is to consider ways of decreasing populations. For much less money and with concern for the public safety, large groups of nonviolent offenders could be dealt with more positively through noninstitutional, community correctional programs. While many states have passed token community corrections acts, these bills have appropriated insignificant funds compared with state prison budgets. If public safety is truly the concern, legislators would do well to consider the mental and emotional conditions of the young property offenders who are released back into society after two or three or more years of survival struggles in the dehumanizing and violent prison environment of today. It is particularly ironic that job placement, vocational training, and educational programs, which are so important in the prevention of crime and delinquency, are suffering at the expense of huge increases in state prison funding.

Some efforts have been made to bolster community correctional programs that are better able to serve certain offenders who may have been imprisoned. In response to court rulings, legislatures have considered some innovative practices such as intensive probation and restitution/community service as possible options to imprisonment. In some states the legislatures have been forced to reconsider the harshness of the penal code in light of severe financial constraints. Additionally, there have been some efforts to make use of various forms of early release. It is mandatory that correctional officials regain some control over the population levels. Without formal and planned legislative policies for easing overcrowding, prison officials will have to resort to "under-the-table" schemes to manipulate populations; these are certain to be more discretionary, highly arbitrary, and perhaps capricious.

At the very least, 1983 suits have been effective in clarifying the realities of prison conditions and illustrating the costliness of the penal sanction. It can only be hoped that more constructive and reasoned approaches to sentencing and the use of imprisonment will be devised. The chapter that follows presents an overview of the Scandinavian approach which many feel has been successful in addressing the above issues. These materials are put forth to provide us with some basis for considering new ways of thinking about the prison problems that have troubled our correctional experts for many decades. It is for the readers to determine which elements of the Scandinavian model might have applicability in the prison systems of the United States.

3. Scandinavian Criminology and Prisons

Scandinavian Criminology

Compared to the confusion and controversy that surround prison systems in the United States, Scandinavian prisons operate under a fairly coherent and straightforward philosophy. The principles of Scandinavian corrections are more clearly defined because of the parsimony and consensus found among Scandinavian criminologists. There is a much higher degree of consistency within criminological circles in Scandinavia with regard to theories of crime causation and the objectives of the justice system. Criminologists in Norway, Sweden, Denmark, and to a lesser extent, Finland, and Iceland, have been recognized worldwide for their unique and progressive writings. We will review some of these interesting works before moving on to consider criminal sentencing and prison administration in Scandinavia.

Lahti (1985), a Finnish criminologist, has noted the harmonization of criminal law and the coordination of penal policies among the five Scandinavian countries. The countries have common historical and legal traditions, and their economic, social, and cultural development has been very similar. With ethnically homogenous populations and the same dominant religion, it is not surprising that a distinctive Scandinavian criminology has emerged. This is not to say, however, that there is not diversity. Snare and Bondeson (1985) illustrate the scope of criminology in the Nordic countries as they discuss the activities of the Scandinavian Research Council for Criminology, which was established in 1962 in order to promote and coordinate criminological research among the member states. Topics for the annual meetings of this group demonstrate the broad range of criminological interests. In pragmatic Denmark, meetings have focused on the relevance of criminological research to policy-making and the role of criminologists in the justice system. At gatherings in Norway and Iceland, debate has centered on conflict resolution and issues such as alternatives to formal social control mechanisms. At the meetings in Sweden and Finland, subjects have ranged from economic crime and Marxist research to "neoclassical criminology" and methods of controlling the police. With this rich diversity of interests, then, one may ask if there is indeed a common underlying ideology in Scandinavian criminology. Most would answer "yes."

One of the dominant, and perhaps overriding, themes in Nordic criminology has been the recognition that criminality is related to the environment and social phenomena, including labor market policy and general economic structures; physical planning and housing policy; and health, education, and welfare policies (Swedish Council's Working Group for Criminal Policy, 1978). The legal system is seen as only one of several important components in the overall process of social control. In a discussion of crime policy and the perceived increases in criminality within Denmark, Brydenshold writes that "Crime has something to do with the conditions in which people live. . . . it is impossible to believe that entire generations are biologically different. . . . changes in levels of criminality must be related to citizens' (particularly young males) position in our society" (1980, p. 201).

Christie (1983) has contributed much to the Scandinavian perspective with his extensive writings on Norwegian criminology. He explains that the value of a penal sanction changes in relation to the quality of life experienced by the general population. He argues, for example, that fines and confiscation of property will become more acceptable as a means of punishment when all citizens are assured of minimal material goods—"today, time is the only thing of which many can be deprived" (p. 109). And in her comments on "current tendencies" in Denmark, Kyvsgaard (1983) sees a prevailing ideology which entails an idealistic demand for social justice and equal treatment. Compared to ideology in the United States, she suggests that the center of gravity is a little more toward *equality* than *freedom*, meaning the socially worst-off can be treated to positive discrimination. The gross inequalities in society are minimized.

A closely related theme in this body of literature is the expression of skepticism about the effectiveness of the justice system in controlling behavior. There are no great expectations that the legal system will be able to achieve either deterrence or rehabilitation. Wolf (1983) points out that there is a preference for use of the term "prevention." Deterrence tends to narrow down to influence by fear only. Less severe punishments may influence behavior in more positive ways: moral, educative, socializing, attitude-shaping, norm-strengthening, etc. Even those Scandinavian criminologists who are sometimes considered supportive of "just deserts" and punitive sentencing such as Andenaes (1975) will comment that there is little difference as far as later criminality whether an offender is fined, placed on probation, or put in an open prison for a short term or a closed prison for a long term. This realism (or "fatalism" as it is called by some) can also be found with respect to the goal of rehabilitation.

Criticisms of the treatment model have been widespread in Scandinavian and international criminological circles. The hope for rehabilitation inside prisons, in particular, has pretty much been abandoned. In Denmark, as we will discuss later, even prison officials themselves reject the notion of treating and rehabilitating prisoners as an unrealistic goal. A major difference, however, between the Scandinavian and American perspectives is that the Scandinavian view holds that this is a reason for using imprisonment *less*. Anttila and Tornudd write, "the abandonment of the so-called 'treatment ideology' in Scandinavia has primarily brought about the realization that there is now less reason than before to send offenders to prison or to use longer prison sentences" (1980, p. 48). The justice system is not expected to accomplish the lofty goals of rehabilitation and deterrence in Scandinavia because criminality and crime prevention are defined in the broader social context. Social control is accomplished, when at all, through general social policies rather than criminal policy.

The implications of this ideology can be seen in the policy-oriented statements of leading Scandinavian criminologists. Mathiesen (1986), for example, has been recognized internationally for his persuasive arguments regarding the abolition of prisons. He has also written that "the importance of improving conditions of life for prisoners (as far as it is possible within the structure of the prisons) should certainly not be underestimated. . . . the dismal character of the prison makes any other policy cynical to say the least" (1986, p. 87). Moderation of punishment for prisoners is also a theme found in the comments of Anttila (1983) on prison conditions. She wrote, "Because prisoners serve as a warning example, the burden now piled upon their shoulders should be lightened. . . . prisoners should have good conditions in the institutions" (p. 116). These statements are especially true with respect to property offenders. As a result of insurance and increased standards of living, property losses are now certainly less harmful for victims than in earlier days, and punishments should be adjusted accordingly.

Bondeson (1977) has presented data that illustrate the negative effects of even very short jail sentences used in conjunction with probation (the practice known as "shock probation" in the United States). Because of the counterproductive influences of imprisonment, she argues for greater use of unsupervised, suspended sentences to moderate the already mild punishments of probation and combined sentences. But even these less severe sanctions are found to produce effects that increase chances for recidivism, although not nearly as much as more severe sentences in prison. Balvig (1982) expresses a similar concern as to the negative effects generally of official, planned crime control policies. He is most optimistic about informal, grass-roots movements where local solutions to disruptive behavior evolve, as in the Free State of Christiania in Copenhagen. Such informal processes are more personal in nature and less stigmatizing. They do not create as many undesired results. For example, in Winslow's (1986) writings on the enforcement of drug laws, we find a related discussion of the unanticipated consequences of official actions. He argues that there are hidden costs and negative changes that result from certain forms of control such as drug enforcement (e.g., the structure of the illegal drug market, patterns of drug consumption, the nature of the recruitment process, everyday life in drug-using communities, users' motives for seeking treatment, the amount and organization of property crime, the nature of contacts between users and officials, and conditions of prison life). In contemplating the meaning of the above writings, it is important to recall a statement by the father of Danish criminology, Karl Otto Christiansen:

> Without an aim we cannot speak of rational means of criminal policy. . . . aims cannot be determined by any rational methods, they spring from value judgements. Therefore, any criminal policy may be rational. (However) a means may be called *rational* insofar as it maximizes the chances that the object of the effort will be obtained safely with the *lowest possible expenditures in terms of money and human suffering*. (1973, p. 75)

This kind of serious attention to the personal and economic costs of legal sanctions is another major difference between the Scandinavian perspective and criminal justice policy in the United States.

Before further comparisons, some comments should be made with respect to the most obvious societal differences between Denmark and the United States. Denmark is a nation with one body of criminal law, one national police organization, one unified court system, and a national department for the care of criminal offenders. Like the other Nordic countries, it is a homogeneous society with approximately 97% of the populace being white, middle-class Lutherans. The Scandinavian cultural and political climate is also very different. As Ward (1979) notes in his discussion of Sweden, "model" criminal justice institutions are merely part of a progressive human service delivery system which guarantees all citizens a certain degree of security from "cradle to grave." He suggests that so long as the fifty states struggle to provide basic services for law-abiding citizens, it is unrealistic to expect lawbreakers to receive very much consideration. It is also unrealistic to expect effective crime control. Criminal justice and correctional policies reflect broader social values.

In the following section, we will examine the issues of crime and punishment levels in Denmark and the United States. It will become obvious that criminal sentencing reflects the tolerance that characterizes criminology and social theory in Denmark. A certain moral climate favors punitive intervention over nonintervention, criminalization over decriminalization, and harshness over moderation (Snare and Bondeson, 1985). This moral climate is often ignored or explained away using various techniques. For example, recent trends in the United States toward harsher sentences are typically explained as a response to increased levels of crime. However, Balvig (1985) points out that similar increases in official crime rates have also taken place in Denmark, Sweden, Norway, and Finland. Yet, hysteria and imprisonment levels have not increased significantly. It may be time for us to begin rethinking some of our popular justifications for harsher criminal punishments.

Crime and Punishment in Denmark and the United States

Levels of Crime

The data presented in this section were collected during a five-month research project completed by the author through the co-operation of the Institute of Criminal Sciences at the University of Copenhagen in Denmark. The major sources of data were official publications by the Danish government and the research findings of leading Danish criminologists. The author also conducted a number of personal interviews with those involved in the admin-istration of the Danish prison system. This material will be dis-cussed in the next section of the chapter. Comparisons are made between Denmark and the author's state of Indiana. Denmark and Indiana are roughly the same size and have about the same number of citizens (just over five million). In addition, the state of Indiana is a fairly "average" state among the fifty states in terms of various criminological variables such as crime rates and rates of imprisonment.

A word should be said here about the difficulties in making international comparisons. All those who have done such research note that there are many complications because of different defi-nitions of criminal offenses, various methods of classifying and reporting crimes, diverse types of criminological publications, and dissimilar terms for sentences and programs. As far as was possible, the author has attempted to take into account these differences and make note where appropriate. In making international compari-sons, there is also the complex matter of cultural influences. It is beyond the scope of this book to address the issue in detail, al-though the concluding section of this chapter will include some discussion of the more obvious cultural factors.

The primary goal of this section is to make initial comparisons between the nature and extent of crime and punishment in Denmark and the state of Indiana. In looking at the most general indicator of official crime rates—reported crimes—we encounter all of the above-mentioned problems and more. However, we can with some thought make a comparison between Indiana and Denmark. Table 3.1 shows the rates of reported crime per 100,000 inhabitants for the two jurisdictions. These data should be viewed with caution, since the Danish use a different set of offenses in calculating certain crime rates. As Danish criminologists suggest, Denmark does have one of the highest rates of property crime in the world. It is often claimed that the Scandinavian countries can "afford" moderate punishments because there is so little crime. Obviously, this is not the case.

The rate of violent crime does appear to be lower in Denmark, and indeed there is probably less violence (Sveri, 1980). Differences in violent crime rates are actually smaller than they appear, though, because robbery and rape are *not* included in the violent crime category in Denmark. Rape is classified in a separate grouping of sex offenses, and robbery is considered a property crime unless personal injury occurs during the commission of the crime. Also, it should be noted that the property crime category is broader in Denmark, although, in both jurisdictions, the offenses of larceny and burglary account for the vast majority of reported crimes. When comparing the capitals and the two major cities, we find similar trends. These kinds of comparisons are always crude at best, and the figures should not necessarily be taken to mean that the "crime problem" is worse in Denmark and Copenhagen than in Indiana and Indianapolis. But the data do indicate a large number

Table 3.1. Reported Crime Rates per 100,000 Population for Denmark and Indiana, Copenhagen and Indianapolis

	Denmark	Indiana	Copenhagen	Indianapolis
Total	8,147[1]	3,929[2]	15,247[1]	4,888[2]
Violent	151	305	267	519
Property	7,795	3,624	14,980	4,369
Sex Offenses[3]	52			
Others[4]	149			

1. *Kriminalstatistik—1983,* Danmarks Statistik, Copenhagen, 1986.
2. *Uniform Crime Report—1983,* FBI, Washington, D.C., 1984.
3. Includes rape and lesser forms of sexual harassment.
4. Narcotics, vandalism, and alcohol offenses, among others.

of reported offenses in both jurisdictions, so that anyone in either place might claim that there is a "serious crime problem" and that "something needs to be done."

A more specific comparison of particular offenses is made in table 3.2. Because the total populations of Denmark and Indiana are very similar, we can compare the actual number of reported crimes. The same general pattern is evident as in table 3.1, with much higher figures for the major property crimes in Denmark and higher levels of personal crime in Indiana. There are twice as many burglaries in Denmark, and this is the property crime that causes the most concern in both places. Nearly one-third of larceny offenses in Denmark involve the theft of bicycles; this is of particular importance, given the extensive use of bikes and the costs of these machines in Denmark. It is also interesting to note that auto thefts occur more frequently in Denmark although the country has one of the lowest auto ownership rates in the Western world. The number of crimes against the person is clearly higher for all four index offenses in Indiana. One reason for the low armed robbery figures in Denmark is likely the strict handgun law and the very low rate of gun ownership. This is also probably a factor in the relatively low homicide rate, as well. The number of reported rape offenses, as well as other sex offenses, has been on the decline over the past fifteen years in Denmark. According to Umbreit (1980), this phenomenon began after the passage of laws legalizing all pornographic materials in 1969. He also notes that there has been a sharp decrease in the actual production and sale of pornographic materials since that time. It is clear that there is a "crime problem" even in Denmark.

Table 3.2.   Number of Offenses "Known to the Police" in Denmark and Indiana

Offense	Denmark[1]	Indiana[2]
Homicide[3]	239	303
Rape	527	1,372
Assault	5,813	9,671
Robbery	1,529	5,435
Burglary	102,625	51,019
Larceny	215,411	128,941
Auto Theft	21,842	19,298

1. *Politiets Aarsberetning, 1983,* Rigspolitichefen, 1984.
2. *Uniform Crime Reports, 1983,* F.B.I., 1984.
3. Includes attempted homicides.

If we look at another important measure of crime levels, namely victimization rates, there is even more uncertainty as to whether there are major differences in crime levels in the respective countries. Victimization studies have been carried out for Denmark and the entire United States since about 1970. As a measure of actual crime levels, victimization data are considered by most researchers to be more valid and reliable than official crime statistics because of the scientific nature of data collection in victimization research. This type of data is influenced less by the kinds of problems discussed earlier with respect to official crime statistics (e.g., different definitions of crime, variations in reporting, etc.). In Denmark 5.1% of the population reports having been the victim of a personal crime during the past year (Andersen, 1985) and 13%–14% report having been victimized by property crime (Balvig, 1985). The corresponding figures for the United States as a whole are 3.2% for personal crimes and 12% for property offenses (*Sourcebook*, 1986). Thus it becomes even more difficult to rationalize that the Danish can "afford" moderate criminal punishments because Denmark is a relatively "crime-free" society.

Criminal Codes and Sentencing

We now turn our attention to the question of punishment levels. There are also problems in making comparisons of punishment levels, although there do exist some meaningful, albeit imprecise, indicators. In table 3.3 we see the legal standards for punishment levels as embodied in the criminal codes of Denmark and the state of Indiana. The most obvious difference between the formal, legal punishment levels is seen in the area of property crimes (Greve et al., 1984). A more accurate indicator of punishment levels is "actual time spent," and these measures illustrate very large differences. For example, in Denmark the average sentence served for the most common offenses of burglary and larceny is 4–6 months (*Kriminalstatistik*, 1986). Federal offenders convicted in the United States for burglary serve an average sentence of 44 months for burglary and 37 months for larceny (*Sourcebook*, 1986). Unfortunately, comparable data for Indiana (and most other states) is not readily available, which may be indicative of the state of disarray in our prison systems. In Denmark the average lengths of time spent in

Table 3.3.   Comparison of Sentence Lengths in the Danish and Indiana
Criminal Codes

Offense	Denmark	Indiana		Category
Homicide	5 yrs.–life	40 yrs.	+ 20 − 10	
Rape[1]	10 yrs. max	30 yrs.	+ 20 − 10	(Class A)
Assault	3–8 yrs.			variable[2]
Robbery[3]	1 mo.–10 yrs.	10 yrs.	+ 10 − 4	(Class B)
Burglary[4]	18 mos. max.	5 yrs.	+ 3 − 3	(Class C)
Larceny	18 mos. max.	2 yrs.	+ 2 − 1	(Class D)
Auto Theft[5]	8 mos. max.	2 yrs.	+ 2 − 1	(Class D)

1. In Indiana, the offense is considered a Class B felony if the offender was *not* armed.

2. Because of the broad range of assaultive acts, the offense may be categorized in any one of the felony classes.

3. Robbery is placed in the Class C category if the offender was *not* armed with a deadly weapon, and is a Class A felony if it results in bodily injury to any person other than the defendant.

4. Burglary is a Class B offense if the structure entered was a dwelling and a Class A felony if bodily injury resulted.

5. No longer is there a distinction in the Indiana Criminal Code between theft for use (joyriding) and theft for gain.

prison for the offenses of robbery and rape are 23.2 months and 17.4 months, respectively. In Indiana, even if we assume that sentences for these offenses are in the lower end of the presumptive range *and* that all "good time" is earned, the actual sentence lengths would be much longer for robbery, rape, and the other personal crimes. Contrary to popular myth, our system does not appear to be lenient in this comparative light.

Differences in punishment levels can also be seen in the rates of imprisonment in Denmark and Indiana. With similar population sizes, Indiana has approximately seven times the number of people in prison with well over 10,000 inmates compared to fewer than 1,500 in Denmark (Vestergaard, 1983). If we were to include jails and juvenile institutions, the discrepancies would be even larger. Only a small portion of this difference is due to the higher level of violent crime in Indiana. In both systems, property offenders constitute the vast majority of prison admittances. The large difference in prison populations is primarily a result of the much shorter sentences served by property offenders in Denmark. If this group served sentences as long as their counterparts in Indiana, the size of the prison populations would be much more similar. In addition to the length of prison terms, a moderation of punishment is also found in Denmark with respect to the nature of imprisonment. We will see in the next section that conditions under which prisoners live in Denmark are very different from those found in the prisons around the United States.

Conditions in Danish Prisons

Two of the central features of Danish society can be seen as characteristics of the prisons also—disdain for authoritarianism and avoidance of conflict (Hildahl, 1979). These widely agreed upon cultural values are said to have developed in large part because of the five-year occupation of Denmark by the Nazis during World War II. Denmark is often referred to as a pragmatic society where the "evenness" of social relations and the disinclination to "take sides" are deeply ingrained attitudes that facilitate the development of a practical orientation. Visits to the Danish prisons and discussions with personnel throughout the Department of Probation and Prisons lead to the conclusion that policies and practices are based more on practical considerations as opposed to ideological or theoretical notions in comparison to the United States. This is not to say that Danish criminology theory and penal ideology are unimportant. They are very lively fields of study and offer many innovative concepts for consideration by policymakers. However, general ideological goals like deterrence, retribution, and rehabilitation do not so dominate discussions. Five of the major prisons in Denmark were studied for this part of the chapter (Vester Faengsel, Herstedvester, Vridsolselille, Ringe, and Horserod). Sixteen persons in various positions at these institutions and at the Department of Probation and Prisons provided information and interviews for the research. Questions were asked regarding the goals and philosophies of prisons, management structure and procedures, staffing patterns and training, inmate characteristics, inmate programs, and research. In all instances, individuals were most cooperative in answering questions. Tours of the institutions were casual and thorough with opportunities to talk with staff members and prisoners alike. All of the institutions welcome visitors often from Denmark and abroad. There is an openness and an absence of defensiveness throughout the Danish prison system which is not characteristic of most prison organizations. Because of the willingness to discuss problems and shortcomings, as well as achievements, one senses there is a relatively high degree of honesty and objectivity within the Danish prison organization. This is only one of the startling contrasts between the Danish and most other prison systems.

Perhaps the most obvious difference in the physical structure of Danish prisons is the privacy allowed prisoners in their "cells." The cells are actually private rooms with a small slot which can be opened by staff for observation if necessary. The barred outside windows of the cells are often unnoticed, as prisoners are free to decorate and organize their living unit as they see fit. Most of the cells are very well kept and indicate a sense of self-respect. Double and triple celling is not condoned anywhere in the Danish penal system. In addition to the cells, the other sections of the institutions are maintained and decorated such that the dulling "grey" institutional atmosphere is minimized. Even in the old Vridsolselille prison, built in 1858, there is a livable milieu. The care and privacy in these institutions is in stark contrast with most prisons in the United States (see Johnson, 1987; Selke, 1985; Snortum and Bodal, 1985). The availability of privacy appears to be a critical element in the generally congenial attitudes found among staff and inmates in Danish institutions.

The other most important physical difference between U.S. and Danish prisons is the size of the facilities. While most maximum-security prisons in the United States have anywhere from one or two thousand up to six thousand prisoners, Danish prisons are built to house a maximum of approximately two hundred or fewer persons (*Kriminalforsorgens Arsberetning,* 1986). Vester Faengsel in Copenhagen is by far the largest Danish facility, housing 550 persons, about half of whom are pretrial detainees awaiting court appearances. The other half are those who are serving short sentences of two days to two months. The next largest facilities are the maximum-security Vridsolselille prison, with a capacity of 233 and the open prison at Horserod with 275 units. The special psychiatric facility at Herstedvester has a capacity of 134, and the two other major closed prisons (Horsens and Nybord) can each house 175 persons. Ninety prisoners may be kept at the experimental, maximum-security prison in Ringe, and most of the ten remaining open prisons have capacities between 70 and 110. Outside of Copenhagen, the arrest houses or local jails generally hold fewer than ten persons, with the 43 facilities having a total capacity of 1,071 (*Kriminalforsorgens Arsberetning,* 1986). The importance of the size factor cannot be overestimated in attempting to understand how Danish prisons avoid the rigidity and dehumanization that so characterize most prisons and other large, total institutions such as mental hospitals and training schools.

The philosophies and goals of the prisons in Denmark clearly embody the criminological ideas discussed earlier. Nearly all correctional officials in the Department of Probation and Prisons have abandoned the notion of rehabilitation as an unachievable goal for the prison system. A broad range of services is offered for those who might request them, but the claim that prisoners will be "rehabilitated" while in prison is not heard. Danish prison officials also downplay the role of prisons in deterring and preventing future criminal behavior. *The ultimate goal is to provide a safe and humane environment in which to serve out the sentence.* Herein seems to lie a basic philosophical difference between penology in the United States and Denmark. In the United States, harsh conditions of imprisonment are purposeful, and it is claimed that prison must be unpleasant in order to deter. In Denmark, on the other hand, the loss of liberty, in and of itself, is considered sufficient punishment. Short sentences are preferred (Greve et al., 1984). Inside the walls, the nature of imprisonment is supposed to approximate the outside world as much as possible. The two primary objectives of this philosophy are (1) to provide a decent work environment for the prison staff and (2) to foster a sense of responsibility among inmates. *Above all, do no harm.* To release prisoners in no worse condition than when they were admitted is the practical aim of Danish prisons. Another reason why the prison environments in Denmark are not permitted to deteriorate is concern about being able to attract and retain quality staff.

Whether because of the strong unions or work philosophies,

prison staff are given much more consideration in Denmark than in most other countries. Erik Andersen (1986), who planned the innovative prison at Ringe and has been governor there since it opened in 1976, emphasized the redefinition of the prison guard role as the most radical innovation at this coed institution. The guards function as shop/vocational instructors, caseworkers, and security officers. Standard officers are assigned to one unit and work in that unit only, although they do meet with staff from other units for the purpose of overall prison planning. These officers have a much broader and varied job scope than the typical prison guard. They have responsibility for the training and supervision of inmates in workshops, for the planning of visits and furloughs for certain assigned prisoners, and for the care and management of the living unit. In addition, the officers on each unit together coordinate a flexible time system so that they have a fair degree of liberty in structuring their forty-hour work week. Guards and administrators agree that this system has been effective in increasing the level of job satisfaction.

This new conception of the prison guard role has been spreading to the other Danish prisons, with a similar impact. Guards who were interviewed at the other institutions also felt that the expanded job definition made their work more challenging and interesting. It also seemed to result in more enthusiasm and dedication to the work, something not often found among prison staff. According to the vice-governor of Vridsolselille, Juul Genfer (1986), staff members have assumed many of the important decision-making functions that had previously been the domain of administrators. With a minimizing of the authoritarian structure between administration and staff, it is more likely that staff will develop a similar noncoercive relationship with prisoners. There appears to be little antagonism and hostility between guards and inmates, although, of course, differences of opinion do occur. The governor at Herstedvester, Erik Taylor (1986), notes that the key to an effective institution is to keep the gap between administrators and staff and inmates as narrow as possible. "Effective" is defined in the Danish system as creating a pleasant work milieu and an environment where the dignity and self-esteem of prisoners and staff are not further damaged. As noted earlier, to "cure" the inmate or to "prevent crime" is viewed by nearly all as a task for the broader social system. The goals of the prisons are more limited in scope, with an emphasis on the internal conditions of institutions.

Along with increased job satisfaction among staff, these management and personnel practices are assumed to have positive benefits for the inmates as well. One of the most common reasons for guard turnover is that they become too involved with prisoners and come to know their difficulties too well. This is a risk in such settings, but surely one worth taking when compared to the usual risks in guard-inmate relationships. Violence is almost nonexistent between staff and inmates, and even the female guards in maximum-security prisons voice no fears regarding their personal safety. Inmates, like staff members, are expected to take more responsibility for their stay at the prison than is usually the case. In most of the Danish prisons, inmates are paid cash for the work they perform (not as much as they would like, of course, but is this not always an issue?). They are also given a food allowance. There is a movement in most of the institutions to have inmates purchase their own supplies, prepare and plan their meals, and assume total responsibility for their financial affairs. Of course, there are some who mismanage their affairs, and procedures have been designed to address these issues. Prisoners also have responsibilities for filing necessary papers and requests, planning visits and furloughs, making release plans, arranging work or education schedules, and negotiating unit activities. Furthermore, inmates have a great deal to say about their living arrangements. As far as is possible, inmates can choose to live wherever and near whomever they wish inside the institution. There is some use of involuntary segregation for disciplinary reasons, although it is fairly minimal.

Programming at the different institutions is somewhat standard, with certain special services offered at some prisons for particular groups of inmates. Each institution offers the typical range of educational, vocational, and social service programs. By law, all inmates are required to work or attend school except under special circumstances (e.g., medical disability). As discussed earlier, many of these programs are operated by the correctional officers, although there are support staff available to provide special medical, psychological, educational, and social work services. The institution at Herstedvester provides more intense psychiatric therapy for those with serious emotional problems and those few prisoners who have received indeterminate sentences because they were found by the courts to be *"not amenable to punishment."* This legal concept offers an interesting insight into another difference between Danish and other philosophies. In the United States, for example, the common rationale for longer sentences and / or harsher punishments is that the inmate is "not amenable to *treatment."* Aside from Herstedvester, the only other institution with a "special" clientele is Ringe, which receives young male and female prisoners under the age of twenty-three who have had serious drug problems. Otherwise, assignment to an institution is based primarily on the notion of keeping the offender as near the home community as possible to facilitate visits, furloughs, and family contacts. Since the vast majority of inmates will spend less than one year, planning for the release date begins at the onset of their sentence. It cannot be emphasized strongly enough how important sentence length is in shaping the attitudes and expectations of inmates and staff members in Danish prisons. Everything is different when there is a six-month sentence versus a six-year sentence.

Thus far, we have focused primarily on the nature of imprisonment in maximum-security prisons, which house only the most serious offenders. A few words should also be said about the open prisons, a topic that will be discussed in more detail in the next chapter. The largest open prison in Denmark is Horserod, with approximately 270 male and female inmates. This former Nazi prison camp is managed so as to minimize the shock of going from freedom to imprisonment and back again. Many of the inmates leave the institution regularly during the day for work and educational purposes and then return at night. All inmates are encouraged to maintain regular contact with the outside world through family visits and furloughs. Staff efforts are geared toward preventing inmates from beginning to view the institution as their "permanent home." One important management practice which influences the operation of this institution, and others, is the rotation of staff between the central office of the correctional system and the institutions. Bodil Philip (1986), a former researcher at the central office and now vice-governor at Horserod, notes the value of having policymakers and researchers informed about the actual operations of the various prisons. An important result of this practice is that policy decisions and research projects are designed to address particular issues and problems that arise. The typical conflicts between central administration and prison staff are not so rampant. When those doing research and making policy are more cognizant of conditions at the institutions, they seem more likely to develop plans that are consistent with the realities of prison administration. There is also greater likelihood that plans and programs will be accepted and coordinated when those at different levels in the organization understand the overall picture. It should also be mentioned that this type of rotation takes place between Danish police and court, and correctional agencies, so that the major components of the justice system are generally more knowledgeable of each other and less antagonistic.

All of this discussion, of course, must eventually lead to the question of effectiveness. However, the Danish criminologists and correctional officials hold a very different view of the effectiveness issue than do those in the United States. There is little interest in evaluating effectiveness, at least, in the way we define the term. It is nearly unheard of in Denmark to evaluate correctional programs and prisons by examining recidivism rates. In the United States, the "bottom line" in assessing crime control programs is the impact on crime rates and recidivism. Did the level of reported crime go down following the implementation of a new policy? Was there a decrease in the number of arrests for members of a particular target group (e.g., career criminals)? This kind of evaluation research is seldom found in Denmark because criminal justice officials will not allow themselves to be trapped into making exaggerated claims of achieving unrealistic goals. In the United States, it is not uncommon for small, new programs to set goals of decreasing the crime rates in large metropolitan areas by 20% or 30% or more. Such unrealistic goals are usually necessary in order to secure funding. Deterrence must be accomplished, somehow. The same situation exists with respect to evaluation on the individual level. How many of the offenders who participated in the program were rearrested? These types of evaluations only serve to perpetuate the myth that the criminal justice system alone is responsible for the control and prevention of crime. The approach breeds cynicism and distrust because the justice system, of course, always appears to be ineffective. Evaluations, when they are undertaken in Denmark, tend to be used more for the sake of planning and coordination. They may also be aimed at answering the question raised by the quote earlier in the chapter: Was the goal obtained safely with the lowest possible expenditures in terms of money and human suffering?

Cultural Values and Imprisonment

Of course, the extent to which prison is used and the conditions of imprisonment are influenced to a large degree by the cultural values and beliefs of a nation. The pioneering anthropological works of Mead (1935) clearly demonstrated the importance of cultural values in shaping the temperaments and attitudes of societies. In her research, neighboring groups were found to have evolved into very different societies as a result of differences in child-rearing and social principles. The Arapesh emphasized a warm and loving environment where close contact with both parents and other adults was the norm, and children were discouraged from showing aggression toward others. Frustration could be expressed against inanimate objects by throwing stones at the ground or hitting trees with a stick. Youth grew up for the most part to be trusting and cooperative adults who valued the friendship and serenity of a peaceful existence. Nearby, in what is now New Guinea, Mead described the Mundugumor society as one which was characterized as violent, competitive, and jealous. Children were treated with indifference, as parents had neither the time nor inclination to teach love and warmth. Discipline was rigid among the Mundugumor, and the children were raised in a world of prohibitions. Not surprisingly, children grew to become adults who cared only for their own well-being and respected others only to the extent that they had greater power. Those most willing to subjugate others lived well, and those who could not or would not oppress others lived in fear.

Earlier, we noted the dislike of authoritarianism that characterizes Danish society. It is clear that the prison system reflects this value, as do other institutions in Danish society. In the schools, for example, there is a much stronger emphasis on egalitarianism as compared with many other nations. The relationship between student and teacher is a more personal one, as evidenced by the simple matter of being on a first-name basis. This phenomenon can also be seen in the workplace, where the distance between superior and subordinate is generally minimized. Furthermore, family relations in Denmark are not based on the complete subservience of children, and the imposition of a disciplined regime is not a priority. The common thread in these examples is *the emphasis on developing an internal sense of responsibility for one's behavior*. This laudable goal may be achieved by resisting the urge to teach proper behavior through the use of authority figures and external discipline. Perhaps we cannot expect youth to develop an internal locus of control when they are constantly taught that they will be expected to do as told by all authority figures, including the mother and father, teacher and principal, boss and supervisor, the police officer and the judge, and the prison guard.

There are many reasons why the imposition of external discipline through punishment so often fails. It is rarely perceived as fair. All kinds of different people have all kinds of different standards for behavior. It is usually not consistent. From day to day, even the loving parent will change somewhat about what will and will not be tolerated. Discipline often seems unreasonable. There is understandable frustration about being reprimanded for a minor oversight because the boss is "in a bad mood." It typically involves only punishment. The rewards for a child returning home at the proper time are probably few, but the night of missing curfew and being punished is likely to be memorable. Strict discipline tends to escalate punishments. Being expelled for three days for skipping school the first time may be reasonable. But what is to happen the third time? Disciplining and punishing generate guilt. Those who are not able to meet all the standards and expectations come to have a low self-esteem, or they reject the idea of external control outright. In either case, the outcome is negative. External discipline is power, and many of those disciplined too often or too harshly are forced, at some point, either to resign themselves to being powerless or to become rebellious. It is difficult to say which is the more serious problem.

Two other cultural values that play a significant role in Danish society are the abhorrence of violence and the avoidance of conflict. Confrontation is an approach that is not preferred at the political or individual level of interaction. The German occupation of Denmark made clear the potential risks of aggressive and authoritarian regimes. In those nations exposed most directly to the violence of German militarism, there evolved a skepticism regarding the force and conflict that necessarily grow out of rigid, absolutist philosophies. Dogmatic ideologies which leave little room for compromise and understanding can only bring about polarization, further misunderstanding, and eventually hostility. It is for this reason that the Danish have developed a strong belief in the values of cooperation and pragmatism. The result is a social system in which violence and aggression are scorned.

Many examples of this nonviolent ethic can be witnessed throughout Scandinavian society. The most interesting example is the law passed in Sweden making it a crime to spank children. Of course, this is the type of law that is difficult to enforce, much like the so-called victimless crime laws in the United States (gambling, drug use, prostitution, underage drinking, etc.). But it is a law that makes a social statement, namely that physical force is not to be used in the settling of any dispute even within the family. The taboo against violence is also readily apparent in the media. While *Rambo* and other imported movies glorifying violence can be seen, there is an admirable restraint among the Danish media with respect to the exploitation of violence. The entertainment industry in Denmark has generally refused to capitalize on the excitement of violence, and the news media has avoided the temptation to dramatize the tragedies and misfortunes of crime victims. The rejection of violent behavior in its many forms and from its many sources does appear to have had an important influence on the societies and the justice systems in the Scandinavian countries.

In concluding, it may be said that there is a high degree of consistency along with a realism in the Danish system of criminal justice. This seems to be due in large part to the definition of crime as a social problem and an acceptance of the limited role of the justice system in behavior control. It is also clear that Denmark has settled on a more moderate level of criminal punishment at a time when many nations are devising extreme and unmanageable punishment schemes. In spite of fairly dramatic increases in crime levels over the past twenty years, the Danish have resolved to avoid the temptation of overreacting and overusing imprisonment. There can be no doubt that the Danish justice system and prisons, in particular, are models to be considered by the world community.

The issue then arises as to whether the Scandinavian model is unique to those societies or whether some of its elements can be made functional in other settings as well (this matter will be considered further in chapter 5). Those hostile to moderation in criminal justice will argue that the small and homogeneous Scandinavian societies are too different. It has been said that the United States would have to sacrifice something essential in order to move in this direction. There may come a time, however, when the realization sets in that our imprisonment policies and criminal punishments are too costly. It is then that we may wish to recall some of the philosophies, policies, and practices from Scandinavia.

Since the basic essence of the successful Scandinavian penal philosophy is centered around the concept of open imprisonment, the next chapter is devoted to analyzing this idea in greater detail. History has shown that the large, closed maximum-security prisons cannot be changed and will continue to persist as one of the most barbaric features of modern progressive societies. Nearly every society recognizes the dangers of these institutions, and they subject only their most marginal citizens to such degrading conditions. The correctional system in the United States has already developed a small system of open prisons geared toward housing the white-collar and middle-class citizens who run afoul of the law. A primary purpose of chapter 4 is to suggest the potential savings, in human and monetary terms, that could accrue from an expansion of the open minimum-security prison model. The following contrast between open and closed prisons represents two very different ways of thinking about how a society might respond to crime and what it could do with its wrongdoers.

4. Open versus Closed Prisons

I was recently released from solitary confinement after being held therein for 37 months [months!]. A silent system was imposed upon me and to even whisper to the man in the next cell resulted in being beaten by guards, sprayed with chemical mace, black-jacked, stomped and thrown into a strip-cell naked to sleep on a concrete floor without bedding, covering, wash basin or even a toilet. The floor served as a toilet and bed, and even there the silent system was enforced. To let a moan escape your lips because of the pain and discomfort . . . resulted in another beating. I spent not days, but months there during my 37 months in solitary . . . I have filed every writ possible against the administrative acts of brutality. The state courts have all denied the petitions. Because of my refusal to let things die down and forget all that happened during my 37 months in solitary . . . I am the most hated prisoner in [this] penitentiary, and called a "hard-core incorrigible."

Maybe I am an incorrigible, but if true, it's because I would rather die than to accept being treated as less than a human being. I have never complained of my prison sentence as being unjustified except through legal means of appeals. I have never put a knife on a guard's throat and demanded my release. I know that thieves must be punished and I don't justify stealing, even though I am a thief myself. But now I don't think I will be a thief when I am released. No, I'm not rehabilitated. It's just that I no longer think of becoming wealthy by stealing. I now only think of killing—killing those who have beaten me and treated me as if I were a dog. I hope and pray for the sake of my own soul in future life of freedom that I am able to overcome the bitterness and hatred which eats daily at my soul, but I know to overcome it will not be easy. (Prisoner quoted by Zimbardo, 1983)

ON OPEN PRISONS

They treat you like a human being. They say, "Enjoy your meal," "good morning." They treat you like a man, they let you do things the way you like. . . . I just can't believe they don't despise you because you're a criminal. The main difference is the attitude of your fellow prisoners and staff . . . the staff in Britain would treat you as, well, "animal" is too strong a word, [but] basically with a lack of any humanity. The way that going to the toilet is arranged, the lack of showers, the way staff would shout at people continually, that wouldn't work in Holland, they'd go on strike or something. If you want rehabilitation, they [the Dutch] will do anything for you. . . . In England, the attitude is "once a criminal, always a criminal." In England, food was dumped on disgusting plates; real plates were used in the Netherlands. Here you can control the lighting system in your room, that's not so in England. . . . very small things make a big difference. They [the Dutch] have your liberty and that's enough. They don't have to make your life complete hell. . . . Dutch prisons are much better, especially, at thinking how to bring prisoners back to normal life. (English and Dutch prisoners quoted by Downes, 1988)

The Basic Dilemma for Prisons

What is the true purpose of sending offenders to prison? If it is vengeance and retribution, or the long-term segregation of violent criminals for the protection of society, then the closed prison is perhaps the most appropriate design. It is neither humane nor compassionate, but the closed prison system of warehousing violent and hardened offenders in dangerous and harsh prisons is not illogical in a purely practical sense. At least, this relatively small group of inmates will not be released back into society until they are probably too old to be much of a threat. This book, however, is more concerned with the majority of offenders who are sent to prison for nonviolent crimes. It may be necessary at some point in time to focus on policies specifically for the nonviolent offender based on the utilitarian rationale of achieving the greater benefits for the greater numbers. Because of the fear and anger that is generated by the violent offender, it is more likely that we may begin some movement toward more reasoned imprisonment policies by concentrating on the nonviolent offenders.

Whatever the rationale for incarcerating the nonviolent offender, policies must begin with the recognition that these persons will reenter society in the not too distant future. The primary issue then becomes how to execute the prison sentence without making the offender worse (i.e., more dangerous) when he or she returns to society. With this issue in mind, we will explore the nature of open and closed prison environments in the following pages. One goal in describing the contrasting milieus of open and closed prisons is to see how relationships and living skills are valued and devalued in the differing environments. Regardless of the official policies and programs of a prison system, the impact of the prison experience is likely to be measured by the inmate in terms of what was learned about "getting along." Upon release, the ex-con will resort to certain kinds of behaviors which have been learned during the prison term. Learning theorists have taught us that our most recent and intense behavioral patterns are those that most clearly influence our present behavior. For a convict leaving the prison environment after even a relatively short stay, the survival strategies developed during incarceration will play an important role in how the adjustment is made to the outside world.

Descriptions of the "prison community" (Clemmer, 1940) and the "society of captives" (Sykes, 1958) have been presented periodically over the years. The "houses of darkness" (Orlands, 1975) have been illuminated in the literature and "prison victimization" (Bowker, 1980) has been lucidly portrayed. The pains and deprivations of life in the closed prison have been discussed often by researchers and writers who have experienced life in the "big house." There has been much less written about the open prison, although Smykla (1980) and Jones and Cornes (1977) have provided excellent descriptions of the open prison environment. The purpose of this chapter is to contrast the closed and open prison environments while keeping in mind the differential effects of such contrasting models, especially on the typical nonviolent offender.

Closed Prisons

Nature of Prison Life

In discussing the nature and organization of the convict society inside closed maximum-security prisons, there are four overriding features that must first be dealt with: violence, corruption, racism, and boredom. Prisons have always been recognized as violent institutions with hostilities among inmates and between inmates and staff. There has been much debate as to the causes of prison violence, but there is little disagreement that the problem has been exacerbated in recent years because of overcrowding and lack of funding. As we will see later, corruption has also been an inherent feature of closed prisons, as inmates and staff both attempt to ameliorate the strains of living and working in the unpleasant prison atmosphere. And while racism has always been a part of prison regimes, reflecting the attitudes of the outside world, the issue has become more potent since the civil rights movement of the 1960s. Finally, the absence of meaningful activities for most of the inmates creates an environment where there is a high level of boredom and a need to generate some kind of stimulating activity.

The nature of prison life is in many ways a reflection of the structure of daily living in the outside world. Earlier research on prisoner subcultures has tended to emphasize the unique features of the prison subculture and the inmate code. There are certainly some unique features. Prisoners have little or no formal power. They are not allowed to vote. They cannot choose where they will live, what kind of job they will take, with whom they will associate, when they will eat and sleep and shower, how they will organize their daily activities, and, of course, they are not free to decide to move to another environment. Given these obvious differences, it can still be said that convict society is similar to the real world at least insofar as some prisoners are fairly "successful" in doing their time and others are not; some survive and others do not.

As on the outside, there are "haves" and "have nots" in prison, and status is determined in large part by the ability to amass a certain degree of individual power. Power is defined as the ability to exert will over others even in the face of resistance and to get things done, command resources, and produce results upon demand. In the large, closed, maximum-security prison, there are different ways to amass power. Power may be based on the physical characteristics of the individual (i.e., size and strength), one's background and reputation, how one "carries himself," the prison job or job location, access to certain desired goods and services, or relationships with key staff members. It is important to mention at the outset that administrative policies and attitudes promote and protect the power structure within the convict society. Prison staff members and the administration are not only aware of the informal power structures among prisoners, but they have a vested interest in maintaining and manipulating the convict subculture. One of the best examples is the way in which the race issue is handled. In keeping the tensions high between black and white inmates, guards are less likely to be the objects of hostility. As guards have put it: "When they are too busy fighting each other, they don't bother us."

It must be remembered that in all maximum-security prisons the number of prisoners far outnumbers the staff. To a large extent, the convicts have always "run the prison" and continue to do so today, especially given the levels of overcrowding and understaffing. Of course, staff members can and do exert their formally prescribed powers under certain circumstances, and they possess the legitimate power to make some very important decisions affecting the prisoner (e.g., placement into segregation units, giving and taking of good time, transfer to other institutions, work assignments within the prison, etc.). The important point, however, is that the prison staff has a "go along attitude," meaning that they do not interfere much in prisoner affairs so long as nothing too outrageous or flagrant is taking place. This approach to prison administration has been widely noted and is commonly referred to as "custodial convenience."

The formal power of the prison staff is further diminished because of the animosity and lack of respect between staff and prisoners and the different perceptions of similar situations by employees and inmates (see Manocchio and Dunn, 1982). This distrust is illustrated by the most basic rules of the inmate code: "don't be a snitch" and "never trust a 'cop' (guard)." The guards and administrators are, for the most part, regarded as lazy, ignorant, corrupt, and unconcerned by inmates. Some of these attitudes may be simple reflections of the frustrations and hostilities that can be expected among all those who are held against their will. But some of the convict perceptions are certainly grounded in reality. For instance, it is a widely known fact that some guards maintain active memberships in the Ku Klux Klan and actively recruit inmates and other staff members. Instances of corruption are also reported regularly by the media involving matters such as misuse of inmate labor, smuggling of drugs, misappropriation of prison supplies, excessive brutality against inmates, selling paroles, and ignoring court orders (see, for example, Crouch and Marquart, 1989; Kauffman, 1988; or any of the numerous prison suits mentioned in table 2.2). Moczydlowski (1992) has provided an outstanding analysis of how the closed prison environment facilitates the corruption of both inmates and guards. Given the lack of educational requirements, the low pay, and the working conditions of the correctional officer, it is not surprising that this occupation does not attract the most professional and dedicated individuals.

It is within this framework that the convict society develops an informal power structure that serves at least three critical functions. First, it offers the inmates a degree of order and predictability that is not guaranteed by the arbitrary and ineffective management processes that have long characterized closed prisons. Second, the inmate organization provides activities and avenues for gaining access to goods and services that may be crucial to one's survival during the prison stay. Third, this convict society allows inmates to develop a sense of individuality, which is essential in combating the self-destruction and mortification that takes place in depersonalized institutional settings, as described years ago by Goffman (1961). Physical and emotional survival in the prison environment requires each prisoner to create a niche, find a role, or achieve a status that will offer some degree of protection from the dangers and uncertainties of prison life. In the following section, we will examine the various methods used by inmates to secure a position within the convict society that allows them a certain degree of power and safety. We will then explore the effects of living in the closed prison environment. There can be little doubt that inmates who are victimized most and those who do much of the victimizing will leave the prison with less likelihood of leading law-abiding lives. The attitudes and behaviors of released prisoners are clearly influenced by how they were treated in prison. Thus, it is important for us to understand the intricacies of the prison experience.

*The Convict Society**

The surest way to survive the closed prison environment is to be a tough individual who is always willing to fight. From the outset, new inmates will be tested to see if they are able and willing to protect themselves. In closed, maximum-security prisons, the law of the jungle prevails and the strong will take advantage of the weak. Bowker (1980) has described the various forms of physical, psychological, social, and economic victimization that take place among prisoners. The key to avoiding these various methods of exploitation is to develop a mental and physical toughness that convinces others that you will not be subjected to harassment. The quickest way to accomplish this is to fight and seriously injure someone soon after admittance. Life will be much easier if the new inmate demonstrates that he will not be intimidated and exploited.

If the inmate is unable to physically take care of himself, he may also seek protection within a group. An inmate from a larger metropolitan area may find support among those from his hometown, especially if he has built a solid reputation during the period of jail lockup. Otherwise, it will be necessary to gain acceptance by a clique or gang within the prison. Becoming a member of a clique allows the inmate to participate more widely in the convict society, receiving important goods and services such as protection. There can, of course, be risks in joining with certain groups, although the risks are generally much greater when trying to go it alone. In addition to becoming a member of a clique, the inmate can improve his situation in prison by assuming an important position in the convict society.

Several different roles have evolved within convict societies that allow certain prisoners to survive and perhaps even thrive in the

*Materials for this section are based on an unpublished paper by Michael Massey. The author expresses his gratitude to Mr. Massey for the many hours he has spent describing and analyzing his personal experiences as a former convict and inmate at a maximum-security prison. His willingness to reflect on the prison years and his understanding of the dynamics of prison life shed light on the many problems that plague prisons today. Massey has overcome the debilitating effects of imprisonment as few are able to do and is making a significant contribution to our understanding of the prison and its reform. He is currently pursuing a Masters degree in Criminal Justice from Indiana University.

unnatural and corrupt prison environment. Most of the positions of power revolve around the regular activities of prison life. For example, one of the most important power brokers among inmates is the banker, because of his role in the prisoner economy, which has seldom been described in detail (one exception is Davidson, 1974). The role of the banker is to make loans to finance transactions of various kinds and to act as a money exchange for the conversion of cigarettes to hard currency. Cigarettes are the basis of the inmate economy as the possession and use of currency are strictly forbidden by the prison rulebook. Most currency is smuggled in through visitors. The currency is particularly valuable because it can be used to purchase favors from guards and other staff members. In addition to currency, the bankers maintain a large supply of cigarettes that may be used for internal operations such as the purchase of weapons or the hiring of a "hit man." The banker has a powerful position not only because of his financial status, but also because of his regular interactions with the other powerful inmates.

The bookie has a role similar to that of the banker. He may also function to exchange cigarettes to currency, but usually he assumes this role only after a big weekend of sporting events. The bookie has the power to set the lines which will be used for betting on sporting events. When betting a football or basketball ticket, one must pick the winner of four, five, or six games with the odds (and potential winnings) going up according to how many games are selected. The bookie will always have one game where the line is termed a "gimme." This is done in order to entice more inmates to place bets. On a good weekend, the bookie might accumulate as many as 500 cigarettes in profits through various betting schemes. It is not unusual for the bookie to form an alliance with the banker, given the economic nature of the bookie's enterprise. However, the bookie and the banker will generally keep their activities clearly separated. It can be very dangerous for one or the other to attempt to move into the related business.

Another major power broker in convict societies is the drug dealer. Drugs enter the prison via staff members, visitors, or the mail. However, because of the difficulty of getting drugs into the prison and the resulting scarcity, the dealer is in a very important position. His role may be extremely tense or very low key depending on the type of drug that is being handled. When dealing in heroin, it is critical to make all transactions very quickly so that the chance of having it confiscated or of being "ripped off" by another gang is minimized. If heroin has been present on a fairly steady basis, it is likely that the bankers will become involved and stash a portion for use in their daily activities. This gives the banker additional leverage in case there is a need to purchase risky services such as transporting contraband from one cell house to another or carrying out a "hit" on a rival convict.

There is another type of drug dealer; the one who deals in marijuana. This is termed a low-key position because most convicts have the perception that marijuana is similar to a Pepsi Cola. Most of the convicts will smoke pot, but it is not regarded as a major thrill or a money-making opportunity. The pot is too bulky to hide enough quantity to make much money, and its use is problematic because it is too easy for the guards or search dogs to smell. It is interesting to observe the different impacts drugs have on the population. When heroin is available, the atmosphere is much more high-strung and the likelihood of violence appears to increase significantly. When a large quantity of marijuana is being dispersed, the entire population is much more relaxed and the rates of stabbings, robberies, and rapes seem to decrease among the majority of the population.

Other power brokers derive their status from the positions they hold in the formal organizational structure. For instance, the inmate clerk for the chief deputy custody officer assumes a great deal of power because he has unlimited access to the most important guard inside the walls, and he has access to all inmate records. As in other environments, having access to information is power. This individual also has special privileges since the job often requires that he live at the deputy's office instead of in the cell house. The clerk is permitted to move around the prison freely and never has to be concerned about the many random searches. One of the most important sources of the clerk's power is that he can influence the assignments of inmates to cells. He can honor requests to have a friend or partner placed in a certain cell house. He also has input into decisions about what jobs will be assigned to inmates, and he often has a voice in the decision about sanctions to be handed down after disciplinary proceedings. As a result of the clerk's close working relationship with the most powerful guard, he occupies a special position within the informal convict society.

The inmate clerk at the prisoners' dining room is also an important power broker. Since this individual has unlimited access to all food and kitchen supplies, he is in a position to become an enterprising merchant. It should not be surprising that special food purchases are a top priority among inmates, given the low quality and poor preparation that characterize prison food services. The dining room clerk is often able to procure pork chops and steaks, fresh fruits, and vegetables that can be sold, and like the bankers and bookies, he may begin to accumulate large reserves of cigarettes. As discussed earlier, this "money" can then be used to purchase a wide range of important goods and services. Perhaps the most marketable commodities that this clerk has access to are the sugar and yeast supplies, the necessary ingredients for "moonshine." The making and selling of moonshine is one of the most lucrative operations inside prison.

Another important group of power brokers is that made up of inmates who have jobs related to the health care system. Inmates working in the hospital, for example, are often able to assist other inmates because of their close working relationships with the medical personnel. Inmate medical assistants will screen violent or belligerent convicts and generally serve as a buffer between the medical staff and the population. The assistants will then have some discretion in deciding who will get to see the medical staff and some input into what services might be rendered. Medical personnel can sometimes supply inmates with small amounts of high-grade pharmaceutical drugs. Also, doctors and inmate nurses can take care of a medical problem without entering it on the medical record so that the administration does not become aware of the problem. This is especially important when an inmate needs medical attention for a stab wound or injury that results from an altercation. If the problem can be resolved without the administration's knowledge, it is much less likely that any kind of disciplinary action will be taken. The inmate medical assistants can also assist in helping inmates to receive priority medical attention at times such as during the flu season when there may be extremely long waits.

In a similar way, the inmate dental assistants occupy an important position. Everyone can identify with the pain and desperation of a serious toothache. Dental assistants have the same kind of discretionary powers as the medical assistants and can help other inmates to receive immediate dental attention if they choose to do so. They can also help to schedule dental treatment that might not be approved through the formal administrative channels (e.g., replacing a gold filling or obtaining a replacement set of dentures). As a result of the immediacy of medical and dental problems, the inmates who occupy positions in these areas gain a great deal of respect from fellow inmates and are typically able to use their positions and favors to barter for the goods and services they might need within the informal convict organization.

One of the most important power brokers within the prison subculture is the inmate barber. The barbershop is a preferred location to work because it is usually air conditioned and there is access to a number of potential weapons (e.g., scissors, straight razors). The inmate barbers derive much of their power from the ability to run "interference," which is a highly defined role in prison. Interference means that staff are distracted or bypassed in order that inmates may carry out certain business transactions. Since the barber can issue passes and set appointments, it is possible to bring convicts together at the barbershop when discussions are necessary. The barbers also have access to the entire prison as they make visits to cell houses, segregation units, and death row to give haircuts. This allows them to carry messages and small amounts of contraband to inmates who cannot be contacted by anyone else.

There are several other positions that carry a certain degree of status and power, although they are not as important as those discussed above. Inmate carpenters and plumbers are minor power brokers because they have access to tools that can be made into weapons, and they also can do work on another inmate's cell without the approval of the administration. The inmate athlete has some power in that he may be bribed to perform very poorly in an internal sporting event, thus allowing the bookie to profit handsomely from the fixed event. Legal aids who work in the "writ room" are among the most educated in the inmate population, and their power derives from the access to and understanding of legal materials. They can provide invaluable assistance to other inmates on matters such as filing appeals, challenging administrative actions, and dealing with personal matters like divorce. Leather-workers may also assume some degree of power primarily because of their contacts with the outside world through the sale of leather goods and the opportunities that arise for smuggling in contraband and supplementing their incomes. Generally speaking, all those positions that allow convicts an opportunity to take advantage of and manipulate the system can be sources of power and enhance the chances of survival.

As we have seen, the convict social system provides several different avenues for gaining status and surviving the prison stay. For those who are able to find a niche, they may be able to leave the prison after a relatively short stay with minimal physical and emotional injury. Many others, particularly the younger and inexperienced nonviolent offenders, will be severely traumatized and leave prison in a most negative state, feeling only hostility and bitterness. Nearly all inmates will leave prison with a mentality that is not suited to life on the outside, and this perspective on life will be more difficult to overcome the longer the stay in prison. One of the most important concerns that must be considered in evaluating different types of prisons is the attitude and adjustment of the convict after release back into society.

Impact of Incarceration

While there may be disagreement about the formal goals and objectives of imprisonment, it is clear that the most minimal result we can hope for is that inmates do not return to society much worse off than they were before. We certainly do not need to have the nonviolent offenders who are sentenced to prison leaving the institutions as greater threats to society. Public safety is influenced to a significant degree by the behavior of convicts who are released after serving a prison term. With the ever-increasing numbers of inmates, it will become more important to consider the consequences of imprisonment as the sizable majority of convicts will reenter society an average of two to three years after their sentencing.

How then does the closed prison experience influence the mental state and behaviors of the "ex-con"? There is no doubt that some have perhaps "learned their lesson." Some will have been terrified and perhaps scared away from a life of crime. Deterrence will have been achieved for them. The lessons learned, however, will have been quite different for others. Many will have learned to survive through the use of manipulation, threats, and physical violence. A mentality develops among inmates that is not consistent with the value system that is necessary to succeed after release from prison. In fact, those who are labelled "rebellious" on the inside have been found to have a stronger likelihood of succeeding on the outside (Goodstein, 1979). This phenomenon is bewildering. It suggests that the value system developed by those who adjust to their stay in prison is counterproductive when it comes to adjusting to life after imprisonment.

Some of the mental attributes of those who have been locked up are catalogued by Irwin (1985). One of the most alarming traits found among former inmates is that of defiance. After experiencing the capricious and often brutal authoritarian structure of prison regimes, there is a tendency to develop a defiant attitude toward power figures generally and an acute sensitivity to abuse of power. Relatedly, the experience of incarceration can breed a sense of mistrust and wariness, especially with respect to the police and others in positions of authority. Irwin also notes the mindset that develops in prison regarding opportunism. The appropriation of materials is common, based on the attitude that if people are un-willing or unable to protect their belongings, there is nothing wrong with taking what belongs to others.

Perhaps the most worrisome problem among those leaving prison is the bitterness and hostility that boils upon reentering society and the desire to "get even." The prison sentence served in a maximum-security facility is rarely seen as fair. Even among those many inmates who accept that they had done wrong and deserved pun-ishment, the brutal and corrupt prison environment comes to be seen as cruel and unusual punishment. The released prisoner also senses that prison officials and society in general do not care enough to assist with the readjustment to the outside world. Witness the virtual abandonment of work-release programs, which have served as the one most important mechanism for preparing inmates for their return to society. All in all, it is clear that the closed prison is not the most appropriate type of facility for those who are to be segregated for relatively short periods of time. In the pages that follow, we will examine the philosophies and characteristics of open prisons with an eye toward their eventual use for most nonviolent offenders. By comparing the open and closed approaches to imprisonment, we may begin to think about the types of offenders who might benefit from the open model and the types who must be housed under closed conditions.

Open Prisons

Philosophies of Open Prisons

Prison reform and penal abolition movements have attracted a great deal of attention throughout the world. In all countries, there is concern about the use of prisons and the conditions of imprisonment. Criminologists, historians, and others have traced the evolution of punishment over the ages and the use of imprisonment for the last two centuries. It has not been a pleasant topic to study. The inhumanity of people toward other people has been appalling. This is surely part of the reason for the widespread interest in penal reform. The concept of penal abolition has been the umbrella under which many ideas have flourished regarding changing the nature of the prison environment and the utilization of the imprisonment sanction.

Penal abolition has meant many different things to many different people. For some, the movement is taken literally to mean the ultimate destruction of all forms of imprisonment and penal sanctions. It is seen by others to mean an even deeper struggle to eliminate all types of punishments and legal sanctions from societies. Some members of the abolitionist movement may concentrate on long-term or middle-range objectives, and others are focused on immediate problems. The abolitionist literature appears to suggest that there is a role for everyone whose ultimate goal has to do with the minimization of punishment and the abolition of the most destructive and inhumane forms of punitive measures.

One approach to minimizing punishment is to discredit the most dehumanizing and degrading forms of punishment. Slow but obvious success has been achieved along these lines. Most nations have officially, at least, banned the use of torture and public degradation from the list of acceptable punishments. Many nations long ago abolished the death penalty and curtailed the use of corporal punishments. These accomplishments have clearly raised the degree of civility to some small extent. Continued use of capital punishment in some nations and the expanded use of closed, violent, repressive prisons are now the most dehumanizing forms of legal punishment. Opponents of the death penalty are being heard everywhere and are likely to succeed in banning executions in most countries in the near future. However, success in limiting the use of imprisonment does not appear so likely. In fact, the trend in the United States and several other nations is in the opposite direction. More people are being sent to prison for longer periods under worse conditions for more crimes. This must be a short-term concern for the penal abolitionists. Mathiesen (1986) has warned that ignoring the conditions of imprisonment during the struggle to minimize use is a cynical policy at best.

The primary purpose of this section is to discuss the alternative form of open prisons that may contribute to the goal of moderating penal sanctions. A basic premise of the discussion is that the open prison is less debilitating and more effective than the closed institution. It is further posited that the open prison can be used to a much larger degree with the nonviolent offender without increased threats to public safety. Granted, there are legitimate criticisms of the open prison concept, including possible overuse ("widening the net") and the potential for psychological repression. However, it is difficult to imagine that living conditions for prisoners can be worse in open prisons generally. The position taken here is that the open prison model represents a positive development in the movement toward more moderate punishments and less use of the prison sanction.

Writers from all nations have presented the arguments for more tolerant societies and less punitive systems of justice. The author is most familiar with the works of American and Scandinavian scholars and will rely primarily on this body of literature. As we will see in chapter 5, many diverse ideas and practices are now being considered to moderate punishment throughout the nations of the world. We need to become more familiar with the broader body of related literature in order to contemplate the possibilities that exist for creating and "selling" the notion that imprisonment can come to mean more than just warehousing inmates in large institutions. It behooves all nations to consider forms of imprisonment that are less destructive so that inmates are not released back into society in worse condition than when they were admitted. We may begin to understand how to advocate the greater use of open prisons by thinking about the rationale now put forth regarding the open prisons of today. In the United States, for example, open prisons are currently used in the federal system and several state departments of corrections. Typically, the white-collar offender or the well-known public figure is accorded the luxury of spending time at a federal correctional institution like the one at Safford, Arizona. State prisoners who are among the least serious, youngest, and/or closest to a release date may also spend time in open camps, minimum-security facilities, or halfway houses. A much larger proportion of inmates in nations like Denmark will serve their sentences in open institutions such as those discussed in the last chapter. The philosophies behind the use of open prisons are similar in all of these instances.

Perhaps the most important idea underlying the moderation of punishment through open prisons is the notion that offenders are not so different from everyone else. Unfortunately, there is often a deeply ingrained belief in the phrase from the old western movies that "it is a battle between the good guys and the bad guys." To overcome the illusion that offenders are a totally different breed is an important first step in minimizing punishments. Karraker (1987) has called for a new penology based on "banishing goodness and badness." This argument is presented by criminologists to emphasize the point that most prisoners, especially those convicted of nonviolent property crimes, are not so much different from the large majority of citizens, who admit in self-report surveys that they have committed acts of theft that could possibly have resulted in a prison term (see, for example, Tittle, Villemez and Smith, 1978). The line between good citizens and the bad ones who end up in prison is not as dramatic as we often think.

Another piece of relevant social philosophy is the recognition of environmental and situational determinants of behavior. Viewing criminality and other forms of deviance in individualistic terms makes it easier to justify punitive measures. Overly simplistic thinking tends to focus attention on personal and individual problems rather than on social structures. As we saw in the last chapter, the Scandinavians have been most successful in clarifying the relationship between social conditions and law violations. There is a high degree of consensus among Danish criminologists that crime is closely related to the living conditions of "desperate groups" in society, especially the young males (see Balvig, 1982). Under certain conditions, it can only be expected that people will become involved in illegal activities.

A focus on social conditions is critical in the movement to moderate punishment, since it suggests an alternative to punitive systems, namely the provision of minimal goods and services. One of the most important comments on this matter came from Christie (1983), when he wrote that *time is the only thing of which many people can be deprived*. The value of minimal punishments becomes much greater when people have something to lose. While the issue tends to be downplayed on the American political landscape, evidence continues to point to the dangers of the "dual society" that is seen as a growing trend (Currie, 1987). More social support for the "desperate groups of society" does decrease the likelihood of criminal behavior and is likely to increase the potency of nonpenal sanctions.

Theories more specific to criminology may also contribute to the evolution of less brutal prison systems. Emile Durkheim stated many years ago that crime is normal and will be found at all levels in a society. This viewpoint is a most useful alternative to the traditional theories of classical and positive criminology. Punishment is the cornerstone of the volitional theories of classical criminologists, and it is not necessarily inconsistent with the "medical model" approach of the positive criminologists. As we move toward a more just and democratic system where punishments are applied equally to offenders of all types, calls for extreme punishments will wane. For instance, affluent societies like Switzerland, which take serious note of economic and political crimes, tend to have less punitive systems overall. This brings us to the question of fairness.

Fairness in a legal system is often equated with due process and procedural safeguards. Basic due process guidelines such as protection against self-incrimination and the right to a fair trial are valuable in moderating the application of punishment. But an often ignored aspect of "fairness" has to do with perceptions of our own punishments compared with those that others receive. It is in this light that white-collar crime is an important topic for those interested in prison reform. The processing and treatment of white-collar criminals offers a good example of how we might deal with other groups of nonviolent offenders. If the open prisons are used successfully in reintegrating white-collar offenders within society, then there are lessons to be learned. Economic debates about crime are probably more important in explaining variations in how various groups are handled differently than attempting to explain why people commit crimes. Opportunity theories, in combination with Durkheim's notion that crime is inherent, explain why nearly everyone is a lawbreaker at some point in time.

Penology theory will be greatly influenced by the wider theories and philosophies of a society. Systems of prison administration today are a reflection of the cultural, social, and political values of our various countries. Part of the task for those who study prisons is to discover principles that may be applicable in a wide range of settings. In the following section, an attempt will be made to outline some of the features that serve to moderate the "pains of imprisonment" in open prisons. Of course, there will not be agreement on which notions are acceptable, practical, or effective. The author's research has indicated, however, that these features do make for conditions that are less harmful inside the prisons. It is hoped that the ideas will assist in the development of a form of prison that is not self-defeating; a prison that leads toward more humane, as well as effective, treatment of all offenders; and a prison system that makes distinctions between those who are a threat to society and those are who incarcerated for the mere sake of punishment.

Characteristics of the Open Prison

There is much truth in the old maxim that absolute power corrupts absolutely. Open prisons are based on the principle of limiting the power of the keepers over the kept. The essential features of open prisons that improve the relative position of inmates are (1) normalcy—making life on the inside approximate life on the outside; (2) synthesis—keeping prisoners in close contact with the outside world; (3) participation—allowing inmates a voice in how the prison is run; and (4) temporariness— insuring that the period of incarceration will be less than one year. It is with these notions in mind that an attempt will be made to outline some of the basic characteristics of the model open prison.

Integration vs. Segregation. The open prison, by definition, permits people to leave and enter on a regular basis, thus maintaining a degree of integration with the real world. Walls, fences, barricades, and gun towers are incompatible with the open prison philosophy. Freedom of movement within the institution is also fundamental. It is equally important in open prisons that inmates are allowed to leave *and* that outsiders are permitted to enter. When the closed prison shuts out researchers, the media, public officials, and interested citizens, it avoids scrutiny and becomes less accountable. The flimsy excuse that outsiders may not visit the institution because of "security concerns" is not convincing. Like other public organizations, the prison must be subject to review and control by outsiders.

Privacy vs. Surveillance. Individual rooms offer privacy. Barred cells are for surveillance. The right to be left alone is perhaps the most basic human right. In order to maintain some degree of dignity and self-respect, all prisoners must be accorded time to be alone and out of the view of others. Even the animals at a zoo are usually provided a place where they can retreat for solitude. There can be a numbing effect—a mortification of self—when people are exposed continually and completely to the peering of staff members. Eating together and working in groups are normally congregate activities and not inconsistent with the open prison concept. However, being forced to sleep with strangers and showering in groups can only be harmful. Coerced medication and treatment, cell searches or "shakedowns," body searches, and forced sexual activity are common events in nearly every closed prison and represent the ultimate invasions of privacy.

Activity vs. Idleness. In the large, closed prisons of today, there is little meaningful activity for prisoners. One of the most common complaints in the suits filed by prisoners is what is referred to as "enforced idleness." It is not uncommon for inmates to spend twenty-two to twenty-three hours per day in the cell. Psychologists have testified as to the devastating effects of this phenomenon. Part of the problem is the scarcity of educational, vocational, counseling, and recreational programs, which has been aggravated with the abandonment of the treatment model. The basic problem, though, is legislation that prohibits inmates from producing and competing with the "free market" outside. All that is left for inmates to do is the institutional maintenance work such as cleaning and laundry, and this work is only available for a small percentage of inmates. Furthermore, the pay is so far below prevailing wage standards as to be meaningless, and the skills developed are generally of minimal value on the outside.

Small vs. Large. It has become obvious in the experimentation with open prisons that the positive features can only be maintained within small facilities. The large maximum-security prisons in the United States, housing two thousand to six thousand inmates, are impersonal bureaucratic monstrosities where nobody sees anything nor hears anything. Nobody cares. One cannot care. The staff are simply overwhelmed. The simple logistics of caring for large numbers of people make it impossible for the administration and staff to be responsive and conscientious. The smaller, open institutions allow people to get to know each other and mitigate some of the tension that is natural between the keepers and the kept. Smallness is a necessary but not sufficient condition for successful open prisons. Many small, local jails serve as examples of the fact that small does not always mean better. The jails, of course, are also closed facilities. It is likely that the facilities exhibiting the most positive features of open prisons will hold no more than one hundred to two hundred inmates.

Flexibility vs. Rigidity. The style of management in the open prison will be significantly different. The rigid, authoritarian style is endemic to the large, closed prison. Endless rules and regulations prevail. There is usually no input from inmates regarding planning, procedures, assignments, etc. A more participatory style of management is preferable in most situations, but in the prison it is even more so. If we are to hope that prisoners will possess self-management skills upon release, it is mandatory that we allow them some control over their lives while inside. To tell inmates when to eat, when to sleep, when to work, when to shower, when to rest, when to exercise, and when to speak does not prepare them for a normal life on the outside. Allowing inmates to participate in the governance of the institution also teaches them the important life skill of negotiation. In addition, there are benefits for the staff with this sort of administrative arrangement. Staff members do not just police the prisoners, but they work with them. Decentralization of power is the most important by-product of participatory management.

Caseworkers vs. Guards. With an open institution and less concern about security, it is possible to staff prisons with better trained and more professional employees. At present, most prison jobs are considered highly undesirable work. The large security force in closed prisons usurps the vast majority of budgeted funds. Funds can be used for more positive purposes when the need for "guarding" is lessened. Some of the Danish prisons demonstrate the clear advantages of this type of staffing. When prison staff are hired for the purpose of assisting and working with inmates, there is a much higher level of dedication and job satisfaction. This is in stark contrast to the alienation and frustration among guards in closed prisons. The rate of turnover for caseworkers will be much lower than that for guards, and this will in turn lead to greater stability and consistency in the operations of a facility. It is clear that inmates are more likely to begin trusting and respecting staff members as we begin to move toward eliminating the security obsession in prison. Professionalism is a concept which generates perhaps as many questions as answers. But there are few jobs of social importance that have not moved in the direction of professionalism. Prisons are the final component of the justice system to embrace the goal of professionalism.

Safe vs. Effective. A final characteristic of open prisons should be that they do not get caught in the effectiveness trap. The prisons are but one small part of the justice system, which is but one small part of the overall system of social control. For too long, prisons have been held to unrealistic expectations that they should solve the "crime problem." It is narrow-minded and self-deceiving to think the justice system and the prisons particularly are primarily responsible for social control. Again, the Danish system is a good example of how to avoid this trap. It must begin with the prison officials themselves. They must emphasize that they have little control over the complex social problems that are related to crime— poverty, racism, housing, welfare, education, alcohol and drugs, and so on. Prison officials at all levels would do well to acknowledge their limited role in dealing with the crime problem. A more modest and pragmatic position to be taken by correctional professionals would be that they will provide a healthful and safe environment in which prisoners may serve out their sentences. When the goals of prisons are more reasonable and straightforward, it will be easier to design and evaluate the system, and the level of criticism will be minimized when false hopes are not raised.

Effects of Imprisonment

The above list of characteristics of open prisons is not exhaustive, but rather a sketch of some of the key features. The open prison has evolved for several different reasons and in numerous different forms. There is no perfect design or exact model. Rather, it will be necessary to experiment and adapt the general open prison model to particular circumstances. The final judgments on open prisons will be based on their relative effects in achieving realistic goals. While the open prison may not turn out to be a panacea for preventing future criminality, it is not likely that those who are released from open prisons will exhibit the hostility and bitterness found among those released from closed prisons.

We have nearly stripped the prisons of the unrealistic goal of rehabilitation. Many are viewing with equal skepticism the unachieveable goal of deterrence. More and more, the honest purposes of prisons are being seen as punishment and/or segregation. Unfortunately, there will always be some violent individuals who must be isolated from society for long periods of time for public safety, and most prison systems do an outstanding job in achieving this goal. Escapes from maximum-security prisons are very rare. If the primary purpose, then, of most prisons for nondangerous offenders is punishment, and not a muddle of conflicting goals, we can focus more clearly on understanding the meanings and limits of punishment. We may move toward a more general acceptance of the Scandinavian definition that punishment means *loss of freedom* for a short period under neutral conditions, at worst. To offer a safe environment where the offender is not made worse is a plausible and laudable goal for corrections.

Part of the strategy for developing more safe and open prisons is the unappealing task of continuing to document the negative conditions and effects of current prison systems. This literature has been accumulating. In the United States, Murton (1976), among numerous others, has provided ample evidence of the deleterious effects of the large, closed prisons that house most of the nation's inmates. The publication of papers from the Polish-Scandinavian workmeeting in 1981 contains similar comments on the generally harmful impact of various types of prison environments (Bondeson, 1981; Heckscher, 1981; Lahti, 1981; Platek, 1981). Most of the research and discussions on international corrections suggest that the prison situation is not much different in many countries. The major implication of this literature is that the more repressive and brutal the conditions of imprisonment, the greater the hatred and anger among inmates. And then most of them will be released.

Experiences in Denmark and other nations that are making greater use of open prisons suggest that the effects of the open prison are far less destructive. In striving toward the goal of "normalcy" in open prisons, the social and psychological isolation of inmates is minimized. Personal and familial ties are not so severely strained when the prison allows for meaningful contact with the outside world. And most importantly, inmates do not seem to develop the convict mentality that makes readjustment to the outside world so difficult. They are not so institutionalized. There is less chance that they have adopted violence as a means of settling disputes, and it is less likely that they have come to accept corruption and lawlessness as acceptable ways of life. Given a relatively violence-free period of incarceration and exposure to a system that at least attempts to be fair, it is much more likely that the inmate will leave the institution with an acceptable set of values and aspirations.

A Prison Index

After two hundred years of experimentation with prisons, it should be possible to begin to specify which kinds of prisons are most harmful and least harmful. Comparative research on rates of imprisonment has been most informative. Research on the nature of imprisonment and the relative effects could be equally helpful for those interested in halting the growth of prison systems and improving prison environments everywhere. This might be best accomplished through the creation of some sort of "prison index" to be used in classifying prisons along a continuum from least harmful to most harmful. It would be a difficult undertaking. But so is the construction of commonly used economic indicators, as well as the crime index presented annually by the FBI. This kind of national and international data base could be very useful. Comparative data can be effective in getting the attention of those who would ignore the problems, and praise for the managers of less harmful prisons is certainly needed where it is due in this area.

A rough outline of a prison index is presented in table 4.1 to stimulate discussion about the creation of a comparative data base for prisons. It will be necessary to carry out further research in order to make such an index meaningful. For example, the first step would have to involve improvements in the record-keeping procedures of prison systems and a standardization of these procedures. This is not as difficult a matter as it may sound, since the American Correctional Association and other groups have put forth standards and accreditation guidelines in the past. It is not possible to develop a rating system until there are norms on such matters as how many suicides occur each year in prisons, what the typical inmate-staff ratios are now, how many vocational instructors are presently employed, and so on. There must also be a great deal of energy spent on determining which of the many potential variables would be included in a prison index. This chore will be greatly facilitated, however, by the fact that the variables defining conditions of imprisonment and the effects on prison environments have already been spelled out in some detail by researchers, as well as by litigants in prison suits. Much of the data required for the establishment of an index is currently collected and would be readily available if a plan were to be implemented. The simplest model for implementing the process would be one like that used by the FBI in gathering data each year from local and state police agencies for the Uniform Crime Report. The national index of crime, of course, comes from this publication.

Deciding which variables to include in the prison index and how to measure them will require a major research effort. Those tentative measures presented in table 4.1 are only suggestive of the broad range of factors that could be considered for inclusion. A primary criterion for choosing variables would have to be the availability of data. The index would come to have meaning only if all

Table 4.1.   Basic Elements of a Prison Index

Points Conditions	Rating
Population:	_____
Under 100 inmates (10 points)	
100–250 (7 points)	
250–500 (5 points)	
500–1000 (3 points)	
Over 1000 (0 points)	
Sentence less than three years:	_____
80–100% of population (10 points)	
50–80% of population (7 points)	
20–50% of population (3 points)	
0–20% of population (0 points)	
Living arrangements:	_____
Single celling only (10 points)	
Under 30% of population double celled (7 points)	
Over 70% of population double celled (5 points)	
More than two persons per cell (3 points)	
Use of dormitory-style housing (0 points)	
Visitation:	_____
Weekly visitation or more (10 points)	
Monthly visitations (5 points)	
No visitation privileges (0 points)	
Use of solitary confinement:	_____
Maximum stay of one week (10 points)	
One week to one month max (7 points)	
One month to six months max (3 points)	
Stays of over six months (0 points)	
Other Possible Variables:	
Time locked in cell each day	
Sanitary conditions (in kitchen, cellblocks)	
Hygiene (e.g., shower schedules)	
Percentage enrolled in educational programs	
Average hours worked per day	
Pay scales for employment	
Staff-inmate ratio	
Medical staff (e.g., doctors per 500 inmates)	
Availability of library resources	
Educational requirements for correctional officers	
Number of vocational instructors	
Use of drugs for behavioral control	
Outcomes	*Rating Points*
Inmate Deaths:	_____
Disciplinary Violations:	_____
Inmate Suicides:	_____

Outcomes	Rating Points
Injuries to Staff:	_____
Court Orders:	_____
Staff Absenteeism:	_____
Turnover Rates:	_____
Recidivism Rates:	_____
Health Problems:	_____
Reading Levels:	_____
Mental Illnesses:	_____
Divorce Rates:	_____
Work Productivity:	_____

prison systems were included. Care would also have to be taken to ensure that the variables were clearly defined and carefully measured, as there will always be questions about the reliability of large data sets like the Uniform Crime Reports or the prison index.

Granted, this would be a very crude index at first. However, in the United States there are regularly important decisions made about crime control policies based on the FBI crime index, which is simply a tabulation of reported crimes for eight selected offenses ranging from larceny to homicide. Index crime is then simply expressed as numbers per 100,000 for towns, states, and the nation. So a prison index would not have to be sophisticated. The crime index is the official definition of the "nature of crime" and could be compared with a prison index of the "nature of imprisonment" in much the same way that crime rates and imprisonment rates have been compared. One of the most important findings in recent criminological research has been the data dispelling the simplistic notion that imprisonment rates merely reflect crime rates (see Nakell, 1977). Similar findings that a prison index is not correlated with the crime index would be useful in helping to illustrate, for example, that brutal prison conditions do not necessarily serve as a deterrent to criminal behavior.

One of the basic problems in the history of the prison reform movement has been overcoming misperceptions about the nature of crime and the effects of punishment. But somehow progress has been made. Changes come in small increments and are usually imperceptible, but the prisons are probably somewhat better and more humane than they were one hundred years ago (Murphy and Dison, 1990). In fact, many prisons in some countries and a few prisons in most other countries are close to what we might call "model prisons." These positive developments in the recent history of the prison reform movement are what we can build on. As for all innovation, it must first be shown that the new approach can be and is being used successfully. This is probably the easy part.

The difficulty is in replacing the old system. After two hundred years, the old prison systems have come to serve a number of real and imagined functions. There are those with vested interests in maintaining the prison systems as they are. And there is an entrenched ideology that supports the punitive approach to dealing with offenders. However, there are new paradigms which have been discussed in this chapter that provide alternatives aimed at moderating the punishment of offenders. These alternative models and philosophies provide a foundation from which to build a less harmful and more effective system for dealing with nonviolent criminal offenders. The analogy below offers one unique perspective from which to analyze the current ideology of crime control.

> The war on crime is the domestic equivalent of the international war system. The ideologies of deterrence and retaliation; the hierarchal militaristic structures and institutions; the incessant demand for more and greater weaponry, technology and fighting forces; the sense of urgency and willingness to sacrifice other important interests to the cause; the tendency to dehumanize and objectify those defined as foes; and the belief in coercive force as the most effective means of obtaining security—all of these and other features characteristic of both domestic and international "defense" systems suggest not just similarity, but identity. . . . People concerned with international peace need to recognize that supporting the "war on crime" is supporting the very establishment, ideology, structures and morality against which they have been struggling. (Harris, 1987)

The "war on crime" has demonstrated little success thus far. Chapter 5 presents some of the ideas that have evolved around the world to help us in moving beyond the old and ineffective model of imprisonment that has characterized the U.S. correctional enterprise. The purpose of this review of international correctional programs is to illustrate the wide range of ideas and practices that are influencing justice systems in countries throughout the world.

There can be no doubt that the time has come for us to begin rethinking our ideas about who should go to prison in the first place and what will make the legal sanction—inside or outside a prison—more effective. The nations and policies discussed in the next chapter have been chosen because they represent the wide range of options available for our consideration.

5. International Corrections

Cross-Cultural Research

In thinking about the future of corrections in the United States, it can be instructive for us to look beyond our national boundaries, as we have already seen. Comparative research in criminal justice offers us an opportunity to learn about the efforts being made in other nations to deal with the problems of crime and delinquency. The purpose of this chapter is to examine the complexities of cross-cultural research while exploring the many unique and varied concepts that are influencing developments in the field of corrections around the world. In this section we will review some of the writings that warn of the risks of comparative research yet extol the exciting potential that this type of research holds for helping to expand our horizons in contemplating solutions to our complex correctional problems. The major part of the chapter contains an international review of practices, policies, and programs that are currently being used in countries throughout the world. It is hoped that the discussion of these diverse activities will stimulate thought about whether and how such ideas might be adapted for use in improving our own system of corrections.

There are pitfalls, indeed, to the study of foreign criminal justice practices similar to those encountered by comparative criminologists in their efforts to explain the underlying causes of criminality. Whether it is an attempt to test a particular theory of criminality or the evaluation of a specific criminal justice policy, research is complicated when we move from our familiar surroundings to a strange and distant setting. Of course, there is the language barrier, which typically limits the type of research that can be undertaken, as well as the review of background literature. Then there is the diversity of social, political, and cultural values, which are among the most important concerns in doing comparative research (Ali, 1986). There is always the chance that researchers will fail to grasp the overall context within which legal philosophies and correctional practices are developed. All of those who have undertaken cross-cultural research remind us that it is critical to view the findings relative to the sociopolitical system of the host nation. It is always possible that the success or failure of a policy is due to the circumstances in which the policy is implemented rather than the nature of the policy itself.

Other methodological problems may arise because of the differences in methods of defining criminal behavior and organizing criminal justice statistics. Even the seemingly clear distinction between violent and property crimes becomes blurred when we find that the offense of robbery is classified as a violent crime in some nations and as a property crime in others. Rape is typically considered a violent crime, but it may be found classified in a separate category for sex offenses in the Scandinavian countries. Arrest statistics, conviction rates, and prison populations are similarly complicated by definitional and procedural variations. It is not surprising that such inconsistencies are found within jurisdictions of the same state or nation and they are exacerbated when it comes to international research. It becomes difficult to generate even a very basic data set that is comparable from country to country. For instance, even among those nations that maintain relatively complete data on imprisonment rates, they may or may not include those persons detained in local jails, juveniles in training schools or youth camps, parolees living in work release centers, the physically ill who may be held in secure hospital settings, or emotionally disturbed offenders housed in mental institutions.

Iacovetta (1981) identifies two other complex methodological dilemmas. He warns of the tendency to view one aspect of the justice system in a vacuum without giving due consideration to the other components. In attempting to study the practices of criminal courts and conviction rates, for example, it is necessary to understand the policies and procedures regarding the filing of cases. If the police system is highly selective in deciding which cases to file, one would expect to find higher conviction rates and lower rates of dismissal. With less selectivity, the expected rates of conviction would be lower. Similarly, an analysis of correctional practices must take into account the sentencing methods of trial courts and the conditions set by appellate court systems. A second major dilemma involves the interpretation of correctional philosophies and programs. Given that correctional ideals are conflicting and overlapping in most countries, it can be difficult to separate out the operative philosophies and the programs and policies which have come about through planning from those which have simply evolved over time as a part of the general "way things have always been done."

Despite this imposing array of methodological issues, enthusiasm and support for the comparative method have been widespread. In his classic treatise, Mannheim (1965) emphatically endorsed a criminology that examined the etiological universals underlying the crime problem irrespective of cultural differences. He put forth a research framework that demands rigorous attention to the collection of accurate data, which is then presented without particular regard to the sociocultural origins. Szabo (1975) maintained that a universal type of comparative criminology is feasible because *any* society will "define its rules of conduct and punish those who contravene them" (p. 367). All societies then are the same at this basic level of analysis, and human nature is the same everywhere with the combination of aspirations and rejections. A further suggestion advanced by Christie (1970) emphasizes comparative research studies that focus on relatively limited social systems such as police officers or prison guards. This approach may improve the meaningfulness of comparative research because it illustrates the respective roles of subsystems within the social control system as a whole.

Perhaps the most important guideline for comparative research was the admonition by Robertson and Taylor (1973) that cross-cultural research should concentrate on the relationships between the controllers and the controlled, between those who sanction and those who deviate. It is with this guideline in mind that the following examples of international developments in corrections are presented. The concepts and practices chosen to be discussed in the next section have as a common thread the emphasis on innovative techniques to improve the relationships between the justice system apparatus and those who are subjected to its control. As

Johnson and Barak-Glantz (1983) pointed out, "learning about the criminal and penal policy of other cultures and nations provides an invaluable source of insight and ingenuity in dealing with crime and criminal behavior" (p. 9). With the crisis situations that exist in the prison systems of many nations, it is imperative that we attempt to learn from each other. Only as we become familiar with a broader range of ideas and innovative types of policies, can we begin to think about and test the applicability of these innovations to our own system of criminal justice. That is the purpose of the following section.

Correctional Practices Worldwide

Canada's Two-Year Rule

In Canada, the use of the "two-year rule" has resulted in a certain basic order for that nation's prison system. This rule requires that offenders with sentences of longer than two years be placed under the jurisdiction of the federal government, while those with shorter sentences are placed in institutions operated by the provincial governments (Needham, 1980). While there has been criticism that the rule results in a fragmentation of services, it makes more sense in management terms to separate offenders based on the lengths of their sentence rather than on the basis of whether they committed a state or federal offense. Whether it be a two-year, three-year, or five-year rule, the concept embodies a critical philosophical distinction. As long as the sanction of imprisonment is used for such a broad range of offenses, it is prudent to at least distinguish between those who are incarcerated primarily for the sake of punishment or deterrence and those long-term violent offenders who are incapacitated for the sake of public safety.

The American correctional system has, of course, made efforts to distinguish between various types of correctional institutions (e.g., maximum-, medium-, and minimum-security) and various levels of corrections (federal facilities, state prisons, and local jails). But these types of distinctions have become meaningless under the pressures of overcrowding. It is common today to find local jails that house federal inmates, reformatories that include "lifers" among their populations, and maximum-security prisons that hold youthful offenders, first-time property offenders, and relatively minor drug offenders. If there is to be even a glimmer of hope that anything positive will accrue from institutionalization, the initial decision regarding type of placement is of paramount importance.

Much of the criticism of our prison system revolves around this disregard for organization and standards. If we are unwilling to follow the rudimentary philosophy of separating different types of offenders and unable to maintain the distinctions among different types of institutions, then we will continue to be hopelessly boggled with the quagmire of conflicting and overlapping correctional objectives. Any of a number of variations on the Canadian scheme of organization could be pursued with little disruption and minimal costs in the United States. Given the numerous and diverse facilities at the local, state, and federal levels, there is already a physical system in place that could accommodate various models. A reorganization might begin with a renewed commitment to some of our original guidelines. For instance, the old "one-year rule" for jails would be a good place to start. Misdemeanants with sentences under one year need not be shipped out to state departments of corrections, and federal prisoners do not belong in local jails because of the tidy per diem fees they generate. Youth centers and reformatories were founded upon the notion that youthful, nonviolent, first-time inmates should be segregated from the older and more violent inmate populations. It would behoove us to return to the principle that certain institutions will hold only the young and inexperienced inmates (perhaps a "three-year, under age 21 rule"). Furthermore, it is of equal importance that those who are serving very long sentences remain separate from those with mid-range sentences. Something such as a "twenty-year and up rule" would allow correctional officials to plan differently for this special group of offenders. Those who believe that it is possible to govern prisons in a positive manner must acknowledge that effective management is unlikely to take place within an organizational structure that is characterized by "disorder personified" (Bartollas, 1990). In order to improve on the administration of prisons, it will be necessary to address the lack of order and absence of systematic plans for the use of our prisons. Effective planning and management rarely emerge under situations of chaos.

Forced Labor in Japan

One of the most interesting correctional issues in the United States is the discombobulated philosophy regarding work. On the one hand, there is a history in this country of sentencing inmates to "hard labor" and expecting that prisoners will be required to work as part of their punishment and / or rehabilitation. On the other hand, it has almost always been the case that prisoners are offered the most menial and least rewarding kind of work. With very few exceptions (barbering, for example), the jobs performed by prisoners develop job skills that will have little market value on the outside. In fact, most inmates in most prisons do not work at all or work two to three hours per day, and the rate of pay is so low that it is often stated in terms of pennies per hour. The only incentive to work may be the opportunity to leave the cell occasionally and relieve the boredom (see, for example, Fox, 1983). For all the talk about teaching prisoners good work habits and the importance of hard work, the prison does precious little.

The Japanese concept of "forced labor" in prisons provides an interesting contrast to the American situation. Archambeault and Fenwick (1988) explain the similarities that exist between prisons of Japan and the United States in terms of formally stated objectives such as custody and control, rehabilitation, respect for human dignity, deterrence, and incapacitation. The implementation of these objectives, however, is significantly influenced by social and cultural values, with the Japanese emphasizing group fairness and equality and the U.S prisons placing greater emphasis on the protection of individual rights. With respect to work, nearly all Japanese inmates are expected to work throughout their periods of confinement. Depending on their classifications and work assignments, prisoners receive both individual and collective pay. Those who work on the outside are placed side by side with free workers and earn the same rate of pay. Like work release in the United States, these inmates have expenses deducted from their pay for institutional bills, and the remainder is put into an account for the inmate; part of it may be sent to the family. More interestingly, the inmates who work on the inside have much of their earnings put toward collective benefits for all inmates. Inmates residing at a particular prison can improve the "quality of life" by performing their work more efficiently. In Japanese prisons, the relationship between work and quality of life is clear at the individual and group levels. Punitive sanctions for not working in Japanese prisons can be severe, including solitary confinement, reduced diets, and physical deprivations.

The issue of prisoners and work raises some thorny questions about our theories and philosophies of corrections. Liberals and conservatives alike espouse theories and beliefs that posit a close relationship between work and criminality. It is either said that offenders do not have the job skills or the opportunities to secure meaningful employment, or it is claimed that they are lazy and unwilling to put forth the effort to become gainfully employed. In both instances, the importance of employment is explicitly recognized. Yet when it comes to discussions about work in the prison environment, we seem to generate more questions than answers. What work will inmates perform? Will they compete with outside enterprises? What will be the rate of pay? Can we allow the pay to equal that of "free" citizens? What of those on the outside who are unable to find employment? How will the wages and profits be used? All of these questions point to the core issue of unemployment. When there is a surplus of labor and unemployment rates of 5%–10% and higher seem to be considered acceptable, it is unlikely that the comments about inmates learning the work ethic will ever carry much meaning. The widely used notion of "less eligibility" means that prisoners are not to receive any form of meaningful treatment or training as long as there are law-abiding citizens who do not have, at least, equal opportunities. Unfortunately, it would seem that this basic contradiction about work in theories of criminality and corrections will persist for some time in the future; it guarantees that the prisons will continue to devalue one of the most important tools of corrections.

The Swedish Ombudsman

In 1809, the constitution of Sweden established the first national ombudsman. The function of the justice ombudsman was to scrutinize the workings of the administrative bureaucracy of the criminal justice system and to recommend changes in procedures and policies (Hornum, 1988). The ombudsman position is part of a larger system designed to guarantee that complaints and concerns of prison inmates are given a fair hearing. An inmate organization known as KRUM and various grievance procedures operate to allow inmates access to official documents regarding their cases and materials related to the decision-making process. Fairly elaborate procedures are in place that allow Swedish prisoners to appeal disciplinary punishments and decisions about sentences to the institutional authorities, as well as to external administrative boards. The ombudsman does not have the power to reverse administrative decisions, but because of the considerable prestige of the office, the investigations and recommendations of the ombudsman are highly important as a check on administrative powers. The prestige of the ombudsman among inmates stems from the fact that the position is viewed as having a high level of independence and a sound understanding of the justice process (Douglas, 1984). There has been some experimentation with this idea in our correctional systems. Success has been limited, however, because the ombudsman has not been allowed much independence. The position in the United States has usually been part of the corrections hierarchy.

The potential importance of the ombudsman concept can hardly be exaggerated with respect to most prison systems. Among the basic problems with the prison systems in many nations are the closed nature of the institutions and the isolation of the organizations. Departments of corrections are among only a very small number of public organizations permitted to operate with little or no independent scrutiny from the outside. It has become more and more difficult in recent years for researchers, journalists, and citizen groups to gain access to our prisons. There are usually rationalizations about the danger inside the walls or the disruption to security that might result from the intrusion of outsiders. These justifications, however, only serve to illustrate the degeneration that has been allowed to take place in prisons due in part to the absence of accountability. It is no surprise that as prison conditions became worse, there was more defensiveness on the part of correctional officials to deal with "outsiders," so the cycle continued. As the prisons become further insulated from scrutiny and less accountable, the deterioration of conditions is likely to hasten.

In the rash of litigation over the last decade, the courts have been privy to information on prison conditions and have generally ruled against prison systems in various "1983 suits." Unfortunately, court rulings having to do with overcrowding and violence are typically ignored through appeals and claims that the funds simply do not exist to comply with court decisions. This situation is further evidence that some form of ongoing, external review is needed. In addition to the ombudsman concept, the board of visitors is an old British practice that could also be pertinent. Although the boards of visitors have not usually been considered as independent and effective as the Swedish ombudsman (McConville, 1975), they provide another method for increasing the involvement of outsiders in the correctional system. As long as prison systems are allowed to operate without objective scrutiny and accountability, the most ignored and mismanaged of all public institutions will continue to be a national embarrassment. The discussions about professionalism and effectiveness in the prisons will continue to be meaningless rhetoric until we are willing to force the prisons to become more open and accessible. Citizens can only become more informed as to the true nature of imprisonment when some form of independent and external comment is heard. The executive, judicial, and legislative branches of government will become more responsive to the problems of imprisonment when the public begins to understand the realities of prisons after the veil of secrecy is lifted. The present boards of corrections that are in place in many states have proved to be totally ineffective as a method of oversight.

The Penal Colonies in Mexico and India

The concept of the penal colony has been around for centuries. Some of the oldest penal practices involved banishment and "transportation." Australia and the United States served as early penal colonies for the British, who commonly sent off the worst criminals to live under harsh conditions in isolated territories. More recently, the former Soviet Union had been known to make widespread use of labor camps in Siberia, and the harsh, repressive conditions in the "gulags" were hauntingly described by Solzhenitsyn (1973). The horrors of the Chinese "reeducation" camps have also been described, with estimates of up to ten million prisoners being subjected to this totalitarian form of "corrections" (Wu, 1991). Given the sordid history of penal colonies, it is with some trepidation that the concept is put forth as a potential innovation for corrections. However, there is evidence that this type of correctional alternative has been utilized in a more positive sense in some countries, especially for long-term prisoners.

For example, the "Tres Marias" penal colony off the west coast of Mexico has been described as one of the most interesting and humane methods of dealing with long-term prisoners. These three islands were used as a slave labor camp for the worst of Mexico's criminal offenders at the turn of the century (Smykla, 1990). Today, the colony is inhabited by several hundred federal prisoners who have long records of previous criminal behavior or who have been convicted of murder or other serious violent crimes. Each is serving a sentence of twenty years or longer. Families may join the inmates after a certain period of time, and the colony offers a full range of vocational training and recreational activities. Within this more natural milieu, there is greater opportunity to maintain basic living skills, increased likelihood of meaningful social interaction, and more chance of developing renewed self-respect among prisoners.

India has also made use of the penal colony since 1952, with one such facility in Uttar Pradesh housing over three thousand long-term prisoners (Bowker, 1982). If administered properly, the penal colony may offer at least three distinct advantages compared with the closed maximum-security prison. First, penal colonies can be much less inexpensive to operate. Since there is little opportunity to escape, fewer resources must be devoted to security, and the inmates can do nearly all of the necessary work, making such facilities almost self-supporting. Second, the penal colony concept can be an effective way of segregating violent and nonviolent offenders if the planning and the use of the colony are carefully monitored. Third, the most negative effects of long-term incarceration are likely to be minimized while living in this rather "normalized" environment. Most of the prisoners with even very lengthy sentences will eventually return to society. The nearly impossible task of reentering society after so many years is more likely to be a success if the incarcerative environment has not been so dramatically different from that of the outside world.

"One Person, One Cell" in the Netherlands

One of the reasons that Dutch correctional programs have gained a positive international reputation is the absence of overcrowding that characterizes many prison systems. For a long time, the basic principle underlying the prison system of the Netherlands has been "one prisoner per cell" (Downes, 1988). While there is debate as to the origins of this principle, there is little doubt that the concept has served as a constraining influence on the development of the Dutch prison system. It may be true, as argued by Franke (1990), that the idea behind the "one person per cell" philosophy was based on a belief in the use of solitary confinement rather than on humanitarian grounds. However, the incarceration rates in the Netherlands have remained among the lowest in the world for many years due, in part, to the adherence to the "one person–one cell" philosophy.

It is not difficult to understand how this principle would have a direct impact on the use of prison sanctions. Perhaps the most important element of the "one person-one cell" concept is that it forces citizens and politicians to acknowledge the costs of imprisonment relative to other legal sanctions. A more rational and planned approach to using imprisonment is likely to take place only with the realization that prison space is a scarce and very expensive commodity. In nearly all other areas of public policy, changes in laws and practices take place only after detailed study of the financial implications. It is unimaginable, for example, that sweeping changes would be made in the length of the school year without extensive analyses of the increases in operating costs that would be required. Yet state after state over the last decade has revised criminal codes and drastically modified sentencing practices with little open discussion about the immediate and long-range costs. The failure to address the consequences of criminal law reform works against the development of any sort of plan to introduce a more deliberate and systematic structure with respect to the use of imprisonment.

Another important aspect of the "one prisoner per cell" philosophy is the tone that it sets regarding the nature of imprisonment. Of course, the adoption of this principle does not necessarily result in a more effective and humane prison operation. But it does seem that this could be a major first step in recognizing the deprivations of prison life and the basic need of inmates for a minimal degree of privacy and self-preservation. The loss of freedom and life in prison will always be difficult and painful. If there is to be any possibility that inmates will use the prison experience for some change in a positive direction, it is mandatory that they have the opportunity to seek shelter and respite from the perils of prison life. This is especially true given the fact that prisons generally house the young and old, weak and strong, violent and nonviolent all together. For those who are unfamiliar with the realities of prison life, it may be somewhat difficult to understand how important it is to have one's own cell. But inmates and guards alike will attest to the problems that are created when prison systems begin to ignore the "one person per cell" principle.

The English Probation Center

The probation day center concept has become an integral part of the British criminal justice system. As defined in the original legislation, the day centers were to have as a primary objective the provision of training in social and personal skills for certain types of offenders for a period of up to sixty days (Vass and Weston, 1990). As part of the probation order, offenders would agree to participate in certain activities on a daily basis in addition to the more traditional probation requirements of conforming and reporting. The actual policies and procedures of day centers became more diverse as their numbers grew. Some were viewed as alternatives to custody, and others were seen as supplements to traditional probation. The emphasis in some of the programs turned toward increasing the "employability" of offenders, and in others the concern was more with education and resocialization. It is not uncommon in the growth of innovative programs that new forms and variants evolve. While this kind of metamorphosis has often been criticized, experimental programs need to have the flexibility to adapt to the realities of different environments and diverse clientele.

One important feature of the day center concept is that it requires approval by local probation committees, and the courts are to be kept informed as to the range of activities. Such a formal relationship between the courts and correctional agencies is essential for the acceptance of new sentencing alternatives. Far too often, unique and potentially effective programs are created without a strong relationship with the judicial structure. It is not surprising that these programs tend to be underutilized and often wither away because of lack of support. The probation day center is an important concept also because it makes use of the probation department as the locus of innovative community correctional programming. Probation is the most firmly entrenched and most widely accepted agency of community corrections, which fact gives it more clout in attempting to gain acceptance and support for new ideas.

Probation day centers are not without their critics. One of the most widespread criticisms is the concern commonly expressed about programs that attempt to serve as alternatives to custody, namely, net-widening (Bottoms, 1987). It has been the case with almost every new community program that it does not seem to minimize the tendency to imprison or effectively reduce imprisonment rates. This has been the major stumbling block for the growth of community corrections worldwide, and it is a difficult issue to address. However, we should not abandon our search for sentencing alternatives and our enthusiasm for community corrections because they are not yet serving to achieve the ultimate objective.

Prosecution Practices in Germany

In most systems of criminal justice, prosecutors exercise broad discretionary powers to divert certain offenders from the formal processes of the criminal courts. It may be through deferred prosecution, informal probation, or pretrial diversion, but the fact of the matter is that prosecutors perform a critical screening of cases that allows the courts to continue functioning through the use of plea-bargaining and a limited number of trials. A recent article by Graham (1990) describes the extent to which prosecutors have been able to bring about significant decarceration in the former West Germany with a planned approach to the diversion of juveniles and young adult offenders. Faced with overwhelming evidence regarding the negative effects of imprisonment, there was a radical shift in attitudes throughout what was West Germany with respect to pretrial detention, as well as the use of short-term imprisonment. There had been a widespread loss of faith in the principle of imprisonment for rehabilitative purposes and an equally high level of skepticism regarding the deterrent value of the penal sanction. This movement away from a "custody mentality" had been noted in educational, legal, and criminological circles and was prevalent among judges, defense attorneys, and prosecutors. An increased awareness of the large body of literature detailing the negative effects of imprisonment reduced the potency of political rhetoric on the use of prisons.

While the changes in German philosophy have been predominantly in the area of juveniles and young adults (under age twenty), the incarceration rates for adults have also been influenced. Incarceration rates, of course, are determined by both the number of persons placed in custody and the length of the prison sentences. Although sentence lengths may be increased or remain the same, the rate of incarceration will continue to go down if fewer offenders are given sentences of imprisonment, as was the case in the former West Germany (Walker et al., 1990). Two related consequences of this philosophical shift appear to have further contributed to the decreasing rates of imprisonment. First, as more young offenders are spared the initial record of short-term incarceration, judges are less likely to hand down a longer sentence as the first exposure to the prison experience. And second, with short-term prison sentences discredited, there may be a "down-tariffing" in borderline custody cases because harsher punishments come to be seen as too severe for less serious cases within many categories of nonviolent crime.

The experience of the Germans suggests that high incarceration rates are maintained in large part because of the ease with which short prison sentences are handed down. Short prison sentences make it more likely that judges and prosecutors will slide back into a custody mentality. The gap between noninstitutional sanctions and imprisonment is a big one, and the distinction may become blurred as we accept what seem to be mild forms of brief incarceration. In terms of prosecutorial discretion, the practice of diversion and the development of alternative sanctions will be enhanced as the use of prisons comes to be viewed truly as a last resort. Prosecutors and judges are familiar with and accustomed to using community programs. The proliferation of diverse community correctional programs in recent years has resulted in alternative sentences that can be easily expanded and readily used if prosecutors and judges so desire. An impetus for changes in attitudes and practices may be the continuing crisis with overcrowded jails and prisons, in addition to the growing recognition of the exorbitant costs of the prison sanction. Given the pivotal role of prosecutors in local justice systems, it is this office that is best equipped to initiate policies to clarify the proper role of imprisonment and to advocate the benefits of noninstitutional sanctions in the sentencing process. The prosecutor could be the key to a more reasoned and pragmatic system of sanctions in all nations.

Denmark and Depenalization

The notion of "depenalization" has been an important part of the Danish criminal justice philosophy for several years. In Denmark, depenalization is taken to mean that continued efforts will be made to decrease the number of criminal offenses for which the punishment of incarceration is utilized. The emphasis has been on eliminating the prison sentence for lesser property crimes and minor offenses against public order (i.e., drugs, prostitution, alcohol). One rationale for this legal principle is the growing skepticism regarding the effects of imprisonment. Like their German neighbors discussed above, the Danish have achieved a certain degree of consensus with respect to the counterproductive effects of imprisonment, even for the short term. Along with the concepts of down-penalization (shortening all prison sentences) and decriminalization, the depenalization approach has resulted in lower rates of incarceration, which allow for innovation and effective management in the Danish prisons (Umbreit, 1980).

Depenalization is a concept that has important philosophical and practical consequences. At the philosophical level, it implores us to think about the value of penal sanctions and the importance of maintaining prison as a "last resort" sentence. As a sanction based on fear, imprisonment is likely to work best when it is used least. When a legal system resorts to the "last resort" too soon, there is nothing left. It generates a sense of despair to believe that we have used our ultimate acceptable sanction so widely and yet the crime problem remains unaffected. In practical terms, the depenalization concept forces us to develop meaningful alternatives to the prison. Where it is no longer possible to use the prison sanction, there will be greater interest in creating intermediate sanctions. More importantly, these new sentencing options will not be subject to the nagging question regarding net-widening. Depenalization guarantees that new categories of offenders will be subjected to community processing *instead of* prison.

Just as important as the philosophical and practical implications of this concept is the potential of depenalization to foster a shift in the way we think about prison use. To counteract the tendencies toward overpunishment, it is necessary to incorporate the element of costs into the evaluation of legal sanctions. Reforms and changes are carefully considered in discussions of other social policy areas based on the availability of adequate funding. It is only in the area of corrections that new policies such as sentencing reform, for example, are legislated without open debate regarding the effects in terms of prison populations and the requirements for funding. Since there is little open scrutiny of the costs of imprisonment, it sometimes appears as if politicians and citizens believe that prison funding is unlimited. It is this phenomenon that continues to make crime and imprisonment such valuable political tools. In the absence of dialogue on the costs of imprisonment, there remains too great a temptation for politicians to exploit the fears and insecurities of a public deluged with crime news. "Crackdowns," "getting tough on crime," more imprisonment and lengthier sentences have been such appealing and safe political positions because there is rarely any opposition—as long as costs are not discussed. We saw in chapter 3 that the Danish system of justice has evolved into a more pragmatic and reasoned operation in large part because there was a strong emphasis on examining the costs and the necessities for prison sentences. There is likely to be much less enthusiasm in the United States for legislative proposals to toughen sentences if it is made clear that the size of prison populations will increase significantly, requiring major increases in the level of state and federal taxes for corrections.

Electronic Monitoring in the United States

One of the most interesting developments on the U.S. criminal justice scene is the growing use of electronic monitoring. With the new technology now available, it is possible to improve the level of supervision for many offenders sentenced to various types of community programs. The National Institute of Justice (1989) has pointed out the expanding use of electronic monitoring, which is now being used in thirty-three states by police agencies, court systems, and correctional programs. Monitoring is now used primarily with cases that involve driving under the influence, minor drug matters, and property crimes. There is a tendency to use monitoring in conjunction with probation and parole, as well as other alternative sanctions such as curfew deadlines, home detention, and house arrest (Ball et al., 1988). The major goals in most electronic monitoring programs are the promotion of public safety and the provision of cost-effective community supervision. Relatedly, it is hoped that monitoring will increase confidence in various Intensive Supervision Programs (ISP) as viable sentencing alternatives for the criminal courts (Bureau of Justice Assistance, 1989).

A number of important issues have been raised with respect to the policies and procedures that are followed in the use of monitoring (see, for example, Gable [1986] and Friel and Vaughn [1986]). As in all diversionary programs, there are questions having to do with the selection and placement of offenders. There is again concern over "widening the net," as well as the commonly noted practice of "creaming" only the best possible prospects who have the least likelihood of failing in the program. Because of the effects on other family members, there are many questions regarding the proper duration of monitoring and the contact standards (how often and when the offender should be monitored). Also, there has been debate about staffing and caseload size, fee structures, and procedures for dealing with noncompliance. Constitutional issues revolving around the right to privacy and Fifth Amendment privileges against self-incrimination have been discussed, but it appears that the courts are willing to accept monitoring at the present time (del Carmen and Vaughn, 1986).

While there is still much discussion needed on the issues above, the practice of electronic monitoring does appear to have an advantage over many of the community sentencing options in that it provides a more effective form of surveillance, making it more politically acceptable. It will, of course, be necessary to keep a constant vigil to minimize the chances that monitoring is misused. All innovative community sentencing options are subject to manipulation and misapplication, although we need to weigh the potential dangers of these alternatives against the known dangers of incarceration. Of the many new community sentencing alternatives, monitoring does appear to have the elements that could allow it to become one of the true alternatives to imprisonment. Electronic monitoring is more acceptable as far as judges and prosecutors are concerned, and citizens are likely to be more receptive to a program that places a higher degree of emphasis on public protection. It remains to be seen whether the widespread practice of monitoring will conform to the parameters of legal and social fairness and whether the use of monitoring will come to be a true alternative to imprisonment. This is, however, one of the most interesting, albeit controversial, developments in the field of American corrections.

Can Changes Be Imported?

The purpose of this chapter has been to highlight some of the successful practices and innovations that are taking place in systems of corrections around the world. One of the issues that must be addressed following the above discussion is whether these ideas and concepts can be adapted for use in our own justice system. At the beginning of the chapter, we read that researchers have encouraged us to continue learning more about the practices of other legal systems irrespective of cultural, social, and political differences. In thinking about the feasibility of actually implementing some of the above concepts, however, it is necessary to consider the sociopolitical milieu. On the one hand, it can be argued that the "mood" is not right for experimentation with new and less punitive penal sanctions. On the other hand, the "mood" is always right for new social policies that promise to achieve positive goals without an increase in public spending. Most of the concepts presented in the last section could be categorized as such.

For many of the above concepts—the ombudsman, "forced labor," the two-year rule, probation day centers, electronic monitoring, prosecutorial diversion, and down-penalization—there is evidence that more can be achieved for less in comparison to the expanded use of prisons. There does not appear to be anything inherent in these practices that would render them inoperative in the criminal justice system of the United States. Granted, certain changes would have to be made, but these changes require more in the way of attitude shifts and policy modifications than in funding increases and broad systemic upheavals. We have seen far more radical changes in the sentencing reforms of the last decade than would be required to implement most of the above ideas. Part of the reason why there is so little in the way of meaningful change in the field of corrections is that state prison officials have not yet been able to engender the support and develop the clout to stand up against the more powerful forces that shape the criminal justice process—the legislators, police organizations, prosecutor and judicial groups, and the governors. On a rare occasion, we will hear about a commissioner of corrections or a prison warden who refuses to take any more prisoners because of lack of funding and space. But even then, these actions are more of a gesture and a statement of desperation than a serious challenge to sentencing practices and penal policies. In order for the field of corrections to become a more equal partner in the criminal justice enterprise, there will need to be continued movement toward a broader based standard of professionalism in the field. As long as legal reforms and new sentencing practices are forced upon correctional officials without advanced planning and adequate funding, prison systems will continue to be the disgrace that they are today.

Following the lead of their counterparts in education, for example, correctional administrators must become more organized and vocal in debates about policies and reforms that influence their agencies. Can any of us imagine school superintendents allowing the state legislature to mandate sweeping changes in the number of students to be served or the length of the school year without *first* receiving the funds necessary for implementing these changes? Of course not. The correctional field will become more professionalized and respected only to the degree that it is able and willing to take greater control of its destiny. Prison management will continue to function ineffectively in a crisis mode as long as corrections officials have so little input and influence on the policy process. In those nations where corrections is a more professionalized field, such as Canada and Sweden, the sentencing codes and penal policies reflect the input of management and staff in the corrections field. If there is to be any hope of improving prisons in the United States, and if there is to be any chance of incorporating meaningful new concepts in corrections, it must begin with a movement to educate and empower those who are responsible for carrying out correctional policies. Respect and dignity for those who work in the field of corrections is the prerequisite to an orderly and effective correctional system.

We might do well to end this chapter with a quote from Hornum (1988) in which he addresses the question of whether certain Scandinavian concepts could be applied to the American system of crime control. It is a statement that might serve as the underlying philosophy for developing a new and more positive approach to corrections in America. He writes,

> Surely correctional administrators and prison reformers in the United States would welcome a reduction in prison populations, more manageable and smaller facilities, diversification of institutions, an increase in the use of community-based alternatives, more sentencing uniformity, shorter terms of incarceration, more public support for correctional policies and a receptivity to innovation and experimentation. . . . It is unlikely, however, that these will be adopted in other state and local systems until we stop arguing that "their" Scandinavian situation is different from ours. Perhaps the single most important ingredient is the political courage to establish a coherent statewide human services delivery system, which can provide the consistency and continuity for crime prevention and control. (p. 79)

Following this review of international practices and procedures, it is clear that there is no shortage of creative ideas for dealing with the prison crisis. The past three chapters have illustrated that there are different ways of thinking about the use of imprisonment sanctions. There have also been many interesting proposals put forth by our own writers for reforming our prison system. What is left to consider are the methods by which various improvements may be initiated in the penal system. The following chapter contains a review of some of the most important recommendations for prison reform that have been made over the past two decades within the United States. In addition, there follows a discussion of the principles of reform as enunciated by the American Correctional Association and a comment regarding some changes that need to take place before prison reform can become a reality.

6. Toward a Moderation of Punishment

Barriers to Prison Reform

During the last twenty years, there has been a great deal of research and there have been many proposals for improving prisons. It has been said that prisons are probably the most ineffective and dehumanizing of all social institutions. Since the first prisons were constructed, there has been a continual flow of ideas for reform. The objective of this chapter is to study the range of ideas that have been developed for improving U.S. prisons and to begin thinking about new possibilities for the modification of modern-day prison systems. Before embarking on this endeavor, some time should be spent discussing the barriers that have thus far interfered with meaningful penal reform.

Given the lack of success over the years in achieving prison reform, it will not be surprising to learn that there are many and varied impediments to change. First and foremost, there is little interest in the topic of prison reform. So many issues compete for the attention of citizens and politicians. Prison reform is not one of the issues that can be addressed with simple solutions, and it is not a matter about which citizens have a great deal of information. Correctional systems operate under a veil of secrecy. They are best described as "out of sight, out of mind." It is also interesting to note that prison systems are perhaps the only area of public policy where discussions are based almost exclusively on unsubstantiated claims and incomplete, irrelevant data. In addressing issues such as sentencing reform, there often appears to be a purposeful avoidance of the implications of change.

On another level, Sommer (1976) identifies the barrier that he refers to as "paleologic thinking." He defines "paleologic" as "primitive, emotionally laden, and outside ordinary rational constraints." It may be that it is so difficult to openly discuss the treatment of criminals because it involves some of the most negative human emotions. What may be something akin to our "survival instinct" leads to strong and basic feelings about self-protection, vengeance if necessary, and a striking back at perpetrators. Laws and legal systems evolved in part to serve as a buffer between the wronged and the perpetrator—a formalized process for resolving disputes and allowing the victim some sort of satisfaction in knowing that the law-breaker received some form of punishment. So to confront the realities of prison life requires us to ask ourselves a difficult question. Is there a limit to the amount of punishment we expect after being victimized? We are forced to define and delimit some of our most basic instincts. How much punishment do we need to feel satisfied that "justice" was done?

Another major barrier to addressing penal reform is the political value of the crime and punishment rhetoric. There is hardly a safer topic for a politician to emphasize than crime. Of course nobody likes crime, and certainly everyone would like to discover effective solutions for dealing with crime. On the rhetorical level, there is very little to disagree with regarding the dream of a crime-free and violence-free society. And as long as the politician's solutions sound as if they will be effective and not too expensive, it continues to appear that there is widespread agreement with the popular crime control strategies (e.g., imprisonment and the death penalty). There are so few issues that generate such emotion and concern, while at the same time *seeming* to have rather quick and simplistic solutions. However, politicians (as well as the media) may begin to reach a point in trying to outdo the competition where their efforts become counterproductive. We are beginning to hear the politician asked how the new prisons are to be paid for, and media sources are beginning to have questions raised about their dedication to professionalism when they exploit the pain and suffering of crime victims under the guise of "keeping the public informed." Playing to the fears and insecurities of citizens may pay off in the short run with more votes and increased advertising sales. But in the long run, society will be far worse off with much heightened insecurity and intolerance.

With these barriers in mind, we will now examine several of the most interesting and important penal reform ideas of the last two decades. First, there are those proposals that attempt to influence prison systems from the outside. Included among such ideas are those that aim to alleviate the problems of modern prisons by redefining the philosophy and use of imprisonment sanctions. These recommendations call for a more direct discussion of the costs of imprisonment, and they emphasize a more prudent use of the prison sanction through a disciplined sentencing process that is sensitive to the impact of longer sentences and more inmates in the correctional system. A second class of reform proposals includes those with ideas for improving prisons from the inside. In particular, we will find programs for improving the operations of prisons that concentrate on each of the three major groups of actors—prison administrators, correctional officers, and inmates themselves. In addition, there are interesting concepts that deal with changing the prison experience through the planned manipulation and reorganization of prison environments. It seems likely that any or all of these ideas in one combination or another hold potential for contributing to the remediation of our current prison crisis. These following suggestions for reform have been highlighted also because their implementation can take place without any unmanageable or unrealistic changes in the basic structure of the justice system.

External Approaches to Change

The Correctional "Free Lunch"

Zimring and Hawkins (1991) discuss one of the most difficult dilemmas confounding the use of imprisonment. Given the fact that most of the nation's prisons are administered and funded by the state level of government, the use of prison sanctions by local judges need not be constrained by budgetary considerations. Whether because of personal beliefs or political advantage, both judges and prosecutors can make extensive use of stiff prison sentences when local interests are not affected financially. There is typically a somewhat more principled approach to the use of local county jails, since the funds for the sheriff's department are allocated by the county government. The more for the sheriff, the less for the prosecutor. As Zimring and Hawkins note, state prison populations increased 192 percent between 1970 and 1987, while the increase in jail populations nationwide during the same time period was only 83 percent. It would certainly appear that trial court judges are exercising more restraint when it comes to the use of costly jail sentences as compared with the "no cost" prison sanction.

There are at least three realistic reforms that could influence this phenomenon of the correctional free lunch. One is to expand the use of state sentencing commissions and sentencing review boards which would limit the discretion of local judges and place more of the power for sentencing at the same level that is responsible for funding the prison systems. The matter might also be addressed from the other direction. It would not be unreasonable to offer counties some form of incentive to make greater use of local resources to deal with the nonviolent offenders. There were earlier attempts at this kind of reform under the California Probation Subsidy Act. Or if the sentencing decision is to be left entirely to local judges, a type of fee or surcharge could be made to the county for the use of state institutions. As either an incentive or a disincentive, connecting the sentencing decision with the cost of the sanction will make more clear the financial aspect of imprisonment. A third, and preferred, remedy for the correctional free lunch would be for state legislatures to adopt a more open and honest approach to formulating criminal codes. Perhaps using a model akin to school funding formulas, the legislatures could organize correctional budgets in terms of projections about how many offenders will be sentenced and for what length of time under various versions of the criminal code. The use of prison sentences would then be determined in part by the level of funding that is to be allocated by the legislatures. Such a policy on imprisonment has been referred to as a prison capacity model (Pontell, 1984). Each of these steps would lead toward a more reasoned policy for balancing the desire to punish criminal offenders with the need to control state taxes.

A Principled Jurisprudence of Sentencing

One of the most complex systemic relationships in criminal justice is that between the sentencing decision and corrections. It is obvious that the sentence handed down by the trial court judge will directly influence the length of time that prison authorities must hold an inmate or the period during which a probation department must supervise an offender. However, the sentencing process affects corrections in many other more indirect ways. Sentencing philosophies can have dramatic implications, for instance, for the judicial willingness to use prison sanctions in the first place. When rehabilitation was a central feature of sentencing and correctional philosophy, judicial use of prison sentences was encouraged for that reason. More importantly, the degree to which criminal codes allow or limit discretion in the sentencing decision is very important. Mandatory sentences may force judges to use a prison sentence even when they feel it is unnecessary. And when sentences are defined very broadly (e.g., probation or up to fifty years in prison for most Class A felonies in Indiana), judges may be tempted to hand down sentences based more on personal whim and prejudice than principle.

As a beginning toward a more principled jurisprudence of sentencing, Morris (1974) has enunciated the three most basic considerations in the decision to use imprisonment. First, the sanction should be used only when any lesser punishment would depreciate the seriousness of the crime. Of course, this requires us to make a determination as to the least restrictive alternative for each crime OR the minimal level of punishment that will be tolerated. Second, the prison sanction should be used only when it is necessary for the sake of general deterrence and then only if it is not constrained by the third principle. The third principle is that the sanction should be used only when lesser punishments have been frequently or recently applied although even several acts of an inconsequential nature would not require its use. Both the second and third principles would be limited by the notion of a maximum deserved punishment, or a punishment level that could never be exceeded because it would be too severe given the nature of a particular offense. While there is a need to define more precisely phrases like "maximum deserved punishment" and "least restrictive alternative," this more sophisticated approach to sentencing would result in more systematic and more dispassionate prison sentences. The link between principled sentencing and effective corrections cannot be overstated.

Detention instead of Imprisonment

One of the more engaging concepts for addressing the issue of prison reform is the substitution of what Sommer (1976) refers to as "short-term detention" for the practice of long-term warehousing. He argues that people can be likened to merchandise that will begin to spoil if kept on the shelves for too long. Even under ideal conditions with adequate air circulation, sufficient shelf space to prevent crowding, and proper temperature control, only the outward signs of deterioration will be reduced. Of course, in applying this analogy to the prison inmate, the primary concern is with those less obvious forms of internal deterioration such as psychological and emotional hardening. The other major arguments against long-term imprisonment by Sommer are that it is costly, inhumane, and discriminatory. Additionally, there are concerns about the political nature of the process wherein longer sentences are typically applied to certain groups of less well-to-do and powerless offenders.

Under the Sommer scheme, detention is defined as a sentence of six months under the above proposal. Each offender who receives a prison term would have an initial sentence of six months with a jury trial at the end of the period to determine if another six-month sentence is necessary. The primary purpose of this jury deliberation would be to decide whether the offender is dangerous and poses a threat to society. Each time the verdict is "yes," another six-month sentence would be imposed. When the verdict is "no," the offender would be released. One of the most obvious benefits of this plan is that it helps us to avoid violating the law of diminishing returns. Many offenders will be deterred or "learn their lesson" in a very short period of time. Those who will be deterred easily need to be discovered, so that we will not waste resources trying to achieve a goal that has already been accomplished. Furthermore, there is the risk that those who are minimally involved in crime will become more sophisticated given the criminogenic nature of the prison environment. The idea of short-term detention is unique because it allows for sentences of all lengths, but punishments are handed out in small doses, thus providing an opportunity to assess the effects of sanctions at various points in time.

Prison for Violent Offenders Only

Besides the possibility of minimizing the use of imprisonment through shorter sentences, the same objective can be attained by limiting the offenses that are punishable by prison terms. There are many ways to envision this option. One by one, we may decide that particular crimes do not warrant such a serious punishment as imprisonment. There is some precedent for this approach, as prison sentences for debtors were abandoned long ago, and laws have been passed more recently banning the use of incarceration for certain status offenses among juveniles (i.e., runaways, truants, and incorrigibles). It is likely that there are numerous offenses for which the sanction of prison might be considered extreme, especially given the nature of prisons today and insurance that minimizes the harm from property crime.

Bowker (1980) has proposed that we apply this notion of depenalization to all nonviolent offenses. Several goals would be achieved by reserving imprisonment for the violent offender. Initially, there would be extensive savings on the costs of corrections, while still demonstrating a concern for public safety through expanded probation supervision. In fact, we might increase the level of public safety by insuring that there is enough room in the prison systems to hold the violent offender until he or she is no longer a danger to society. There would be no need for early release programs. This approach to prison reform would also lessen the "contamination effect." By not housing the young, nonviolent offender with the older, hardened convicts, we would avoid many of the problems that result from our current situation where the minor offender becomes worse and more of a threat to society after release. Victimization would also be minimized once the weaker inmates were removed from prison; the stronger prisoners are less likely to prey upon other violent inmates.

By far the most important outcome of a policy to limit imprisonment to the violent offender would be the stimulation of community corrections development. As long as community corrections is viewed as an ancillary sanction, the meaningful growth of community programs for offenders will be retarded. It has already been shown that innovative community alternatives like intensive probation supervision and house arrest/electronic monitoring can be effective and cost-efficient (Champion, 1990). We have only begun to explore the potential of these and other alternatives to imprisonment, and their utilization can be broadened to include even other groups of offenders in the nonviolent categories in particular. Relatedly, the improvement of social services generally would be expedited as more funds are freed up as a result of smaller and less expensive prison systems. Finally, the prisons would become more amenable to internal reform with fewer inmates and less crowded conditions.

Improvements from Within

Bureaucratic Control

It should not come as a surprise that one of the most common suggestions for the internal reform of prisons over the last century has been the "better management" perspective. One of the most recent examples of this approach is the model advocated by DiIulio (1987). The prison is to be viewed as a mini-government. With the laudable concern for making the prisons safer places, the major culprit in the ineffective and violent prison is seen as a lax form of administration. From this viewpoint, the immediate challenges are to develop dynamic correctional leadership and administrative stability along with a strong organizational structure characterized by clear bureaucratic regulations and paramilitary operations. According to the Weberian model, the prison organization would be structured in a rigid hierarchical manner with a one-way flow of information (downward) and would have a clear division of labor and an impersonal set of relations based on discipline and detailed rules, regulations, and procedures. The basic operational credo under this type of management is to do things "by the book."

In the properly structured and managed prison organization, prison workers would be expected to develop a strong sense of mission and high levels of morale and dedication. Their complex tasks would be simplified, since "prison officers would behave according to a manageable number of simple operational rules" (p. 239). The system of order and discipline that would be created would be fair and nondiscriminatory, as prison workers would have little or no discretion. The bureaucratic road to improvement has always been appealing because of its seeming simplicity and emphasis on order, as well as discipline. It was the cornerstone of the police professionalism movement of the 1950s and 1960s, and similar principles have been advocated throughout most of the twentieth century within the field of corrections. Bureaucratization, however, has always seemed to work best when the goals of an organization are clearly defined and agreed upon and when the work activities required to achieve the goals are relatively simple and straightforward (e.g., auto assembly lines). Unfortunately, in the field of criminal justice and those other fields that deal with "people problems," the goals are rarely unambiguous and work activities are seldom simple.

The basic problem in applying the bureaucratic model of management to prisons is that the approach ignores the structural aspects of the problem. Similar to police organizations, where officers carry out much of their work outside the watchful eye of supervisors, it is difficult to implement the bureaucratic model of "going by the book" in prisons, because security staff often work away from and out of contact with administrative supervisors. There is also the basic obstacle of continued lack of adequate funding and staffing. Improved management alone is not likely to solve the prison crisis without other significant changes in the justice system. Better management has been heralded for well over a century, and we have yet to see any significant examples of successful large, closed, maximum-security prisons.

Inmate Governance

The missing ingredient in many of the "better management" models is the inmate. In the proposal above, it was said that the prison should be viewed as a mini-government, although there is very little recognition of the role to be played by the governed—the inmates. In order for better administration to succeed, it will probably be necessary to devise a system by which the inmates have some opportunity for input into the decision-making process. Various models have been outlined for creating a system whereby inmate participation can be solicited *and* used for the improvement of the prison (Murton, 1976). The rationale for allowing some degree of inmate governance is the same as the rationale for using democratic procedures in other institutions. Any chance that prisoners will gain something positive from a prison sentence is increased to the extent that they are encouraged to take responsibility for their behavior and accept the obligations that go along with increased participation in democratic systems. Inmate participation in governance is a first step toward achieving these goals.

A great deal of the hostility and bitterness found among prisoners is the result of what is perceived to be arbitrary and unfair treatment by staff members. The idea of permitting the inmates to play a role in the management of the institution is one that is relatively simple to institute. Regardless of the efforts to improve prison programs, there is likely to be little success as long as inmates feel threatened because of their powerlessness. As has been noted,

> . . . benefits are realized only when convicts spend their time in a setting that is safe and not excessively mean, deprived, and arbitrary, and has resources, meaningful options, and freedom to choose and plan so that they may pull themselves together and improve themselves. Privacy, some educational and vocational training resources, and voluntary systems of change (for example, individual therapy, group therapy, TM, yoga or whatever prisoners believe to be effective) should be available. The benefits are reduced or disappear if convicts are constantly confronted with murderous violence and whimsical, arbitrary and malicious control practices. (Irwin, 1980, p. 240)

The physical conditions inside prisons are important, but most of the literature suggests that the more important matter is the way in which prisoners are dealt with on a one-to-one personal level. We could not be more hypocritical than to say inmates should be prepared to live a responsible life after prison when they have had no opportunity to learn to be responsible during their prison stay.

The Ecology of Prison Survival

One of the more interesting areas of discussion with respect to the internal reform of prisons is the ecological analysis that focuses on improving the "matches" between inmates and their prison environments. In the writings of Johnson (1987), we find the basic philosophy behind this notion of prison reform. Based on the original research of Toch (1977), the ecological approach builds on the assumption that individual inmates differ insofar as their needs and concerns within the prison culture. It is suggested that the prison can be compartmentalized in order to create various environments that will be more or less compatible with the attitudes and goals of different categories of offenders. One of the common survival techniques among many prisoners has always been to try to find a "niche" within the institution where they can establish normal relationships with some staff members and/or fellow inmates. The essence of Johnson's proposal is to structure this practice in a more formal manner.

An ecological approach to prison reform would begin with a "mapping" of the prison environment to locate the various enclaves that already exist. These enclaves are typically found in areas such as the workshops, libraries, classrooms, or recreational spots. Perhaps the key ingredient in this process is the testing and classification of inmates to determine their psychological and emotional characteristics. One of the questions about such an endeavor is whether most prisoners are not very similar, at least, in their basic psychological needs for physical safety and some form of meaningful daily activity. Nevertheless, following classification, there would be placement and orientation in one of the several niches within the prison. Another question has to do with the feasibility of actually creating significantly different kinds of environments inside a maximum-security prison. The ultimate goal is to improve the "man-environment match" in order that prisoners will be able to cope more maturely (see Parisi, 1982), learn new ways of handling stress and resolving conflict, and develop principled self-governing modes of behavior. This approach to prison reform is likely to be most successful in those institutions with smaller numbers of inmates and more adequate funding and staffing levels.

We will now shift our attention to looking at how consistent the various reforms are with the basic principles that have been at the heart of the field of corrections for over one hundred years. The purpose of the following discussion is to remind the reader that the current imbroglio in corrections is not because of an absence of historical ideals and values in the correctional field. All too often, blame for prison crises is placed with commissioners of corrections, prison wardens, and other correctional workers. Many of the critics of our prison systems seem to believe that the field of corrections is not grounded in sound theory and lacks a thoughtful philosophical foundation. This could not be further from the truth. There is a long tradition of thinking and rethinking the dilemmas and challenges that face corrections. Some of the nation's most famous criminologists and best-known correctional experts have grappled with the shortcomings and impediments to meaningful correctional practice. As we will see, the acknowledgement of and adherence to the most recent set of official correctional principles would be sufficient to move the field of corrections toward a more enlightened level.

Principles of Reform

The most basic guidelines for the administration of prisons have been in place since 1870. The American Correctional Association developed a set of principles well over a century ago to guide prison administrators and prison staff in their mission to create effective correctional practices. Table 6.1 contains the revised principles as outlined by the American Correctional Association in 1982. A thorough examination of this "Declaration of Principles" reveals a clear roadmap to prison reform. Nearly all of the most important concepts and philosophies for improving prisons in a significant manner are enunciated in this document.

In the preamble and article I.1, for example, the most essential principle of reform is stated and reiterated—*a recognition of and respect for human dignity and worth*. Since the structure of the large, closed prison is impersonal and highly regimented, the maintenance of self-respect and human dignity is compromised from the outset. In order for prison staff to demonstrate respect for the worth and dignity of inmates, operations must allow for the consideration of individual problems and needs. Resources must be available to provide the basic necessities of life, including food, shelter, hygiene, and privacy. We know that in any situation where basic needs are not being met, there is difficulty in affirming the dignity and worth of people. In prisons, this matter is a double-edged sword. Prisoners

are degraded and stripped of their dignity when they live under inhumane conditions, and prison staff are similarly dehumanized
when they are forced to preside over conditions that are anathema
to the most basic correctional principles.

The quote below describes the "double-degradation" and the psy-
chic consequences of assuming ownership of another being through
the taking away of freedom.

> When a man confines an animal in a cage, he assumes ownership
> of that animal. But an animal is an individual; it cannot be owned.
> When a man tries to own an individual, whether that individual
> be another man, an animal or even a tree, he suffers the psychic
> consequences of an unnatural act. Have you ever watched the
> visitors at a menagerie or zoo—the fools they make of themselves,
> the way they leer and snigger and vex and demand entertainment
> and taunt? A caged beast, like an excess of alcohol, reverts man
> to his most banal dimensions. And he is only slightly better
> behaved when observing human inmates in prisons and institu-
> tions. A creature, human or otherwise, that has had its freedom
> compromised has been degraded. In a subconscious reaction that
> combines guilt, fear and contempt, the keepers of the caged—
> even the observers of the caged—are degraded themselves. The
> cage is a double degrader. Any bar, whether concrete or intan-
> gible, that stands between a living thing and its liberty is a
> communicable perversity, dangerous to the sanity of everyone
> concerned. (Robins, 1971, p. 70)

It is suggested here that the most basic of the ACA principles may
be in danger of violation whenever prison systems are based primarily on the use of closed prisons and caging institutions.

The basic precepts of correctional principles are further specified
in article I.3, which accords the offender the *protection of recognized standards of safety, humaneness and due process*. If there is
to be any respect for the prison system or any realistic belief that
prisons can accomplish something positive, violence and brutality
cannot be allowed to flourish within the institutions as they now
do (Braswell et al., 1985). It is not only hypocritical on the one
hand, but cynical on the other hand, to claim that the nonviolent
offender (or even the violent one) is to be taught respect for the
person and property in an environment where personal safety is

Table 6.1.   A Roadmap to Prison Reform

ACA DECLARATION OF PRINCIPLES

Preamble:

More than a century ago, in 1870, leaders in American corrections first developed principles stating the ideas and objectives underlying the practice of their profession.

As members of the American Correctional Association, we continue in the spirit of our founders by renewing and revising these principles in 1982, so they may continue to guide sound correctional practices, make clear our philosophy and aims, and facilitate our seeking out and involving the leaders and citizens of the communities we serve.

The role of corrections is to assist in the prevention and control of delinquency and crime. We believe that the principles stated herein provide the conceptual foundation for correctional policy that will increase that contribution. Ultimately, however, preventing criminal and delinquent behavior depends in large measure on the will of the individual and the constructive qualities of society and its basic institutions—family, school, religion, and government.

Social order in a democratic society depends on full recognition of individual human worth and dignity. Thus, in all its aspects, corrections must be measured against standards of fairness and humanity. We share with the rest of the juvenile and criminal justice systems the obligation to balance the protection of individuals against excessive restrictions.

Finally, we are committed to conducting corrections in a manner reflecting rational planning and effective administration as measured by recognized professional standards.

Principles: Article I—Basic Precepts

1. Laws and administrative policies and systems stemming from them shall be based on respect for human dignity and worth with recognition that hope is essential to humane and just programs.
2. Victims, witnesses, and all other citizens who come in contact with the criminal justice system shall receive fair, concerned consideration and assistance including restitution and/or compensation when appropriate.
3. The accused or convicted offender shall be accorded the protection of recognized standards of safety, humaneness, and due process. Individuals who are neither accused nor charged with criminal offenses should be served by other systems.
4. Sanctions imposed by the court shall be commensurate with the seriousness of the offense and take into account the past criminal history and extent of the offender's participation in the crime. Unwarranted disparity, undue length of sentences, and rigid sentencing structures are an injustice to society and the offender and create circumstances that are not in the best interest of mercy, justice, or public protection.
5. The least restrictive means of control and supervision consistent with public safety shall be used. Use of institutions for control and supervision of pretrial detention and post-conviction dispositions shall be based on judicious and restricted use of a limited resource. Incarceration shall only be used with juveniles or adults charged with or convicted of criminal offenses and for whom no other alternative disposition is safe or acceptable to society.

Table 6.1.—Continued

6.   Juvenile and adult correctional agencies, whether federal, state, or local, or public, private, or voluntary, must regard themselves as part of a highly integrated larger system that must work together toward common goals.
7.   Correctional agencies, in order to be accountable to and receive strong support from all branches of government and the public at large, must take an active role in setting future direction and must provide information on which public policy decisions can be made.

Article II—Programs and Services
8.   Correctional programs at all levels of government require a careful balance of community and institutional services that provide a range of effective, just, humane, and safe options for handling adult and juvenile offenders. These services shall meet accepted professional standards and be accredited where appropriate.
9.   Correctional agencies shall provide classification systems for determining placement, degree of supervision, and programming that afford differential controls and services for adult and juvenile offenders. These systems shall be based on sound theory and empirical knowledge of human behavior, giving consideration to such factors as age, sex, physical and mental conditions, and the nature of the offense.
10. All offenders, whether in the community or in institutions, shall be afforded the opportunity to engage in productive work and participate in programs including educational, vocational training, religious, counseling, constructive use of leisure time, and other activities that will enhance self-worth, community integration, and economic status.

Article III—Personnel
11. Adequately trained and well-supervised volunteers are essential adjuncts to effective delivery of services to adult and juvenile offenders at all stages of the correctional process.
12. Leadership selection for correctional agencies at all levels, public and private, shall be on the basis of merit without regard for political affiliation, race, sex, or religion, with tenure assured as long as there is demonstrated competent performance and compliance with professional and ethical standards.
13. The staff of correctional systems must be professionally competent and well-trained. They shall be selected and retained on the basis of merit without regard to political affiliation, race, sex, or religion and afforded training, career development experiences, and remuneration commensurate with job requirements and performance.

Article IV—Advancement of Knowledge
14. Correctional agencies have a continuing responsibility to promote, sponsor, and participate in research and program evaluation efforts. Doing so will contribute to both an understanding of the prevention and control of delinquent and criminal behavior and to assessment of the effectiveness and efficiency of programs and services.

Source: Harry E. Allen and Clifford E. Simonsen. *Corrections in America* (6th ed.). New York: Macmillan Publishing Company, 1992.

ignored. In a similar vein, respect for the laws and norms of society is not built within a situation where due process and fairness are often neglected in disciplinary actions and release decisions. Another basic precept from the ACA declaration is that *sanctions shall be commensurate with the seriousness of the crime*. The issue of fairness then also arises when inmates see and hear and read about the sentences that are imposed on certain classes of criminals and particular types of crime, such as white-collar or political. It seems to many inmates that their relatively minor property crimes were treated much more harshly than the multi-million-dollar crimes of the rich and powerful junk bond thieves or savings and loan swindlers.

Article II of the "Principles" is the long-standing axiom in corrections that there must be some positive component in the handling of offenders. It is stated that *all offenders shall be afforded the opportunity to engage in productive work and participate in programs*. This element of correctional philosophy has always been difficult to maintain. With a lack of interest and inadequate funding, prison officials have rarely had the "luxury" of hiring counselors, vocational instructors, teachers, and others who could provide opportunities for inmates who seek self-improvement. The security needs in prison are always the top priority, and they receive even more attention (and funding) as the prisons become more troubled. However, if prisons are ever to evolve into more constructive social institutions, they will have to strive to push the affirmative principles of corrections to the forefront.

Of course, programs and philosophies are only a part of the equation for solving correctional problems. It is clear from the American Correctional Association standards that the matter of personnel is a preeminent concern. It is declared in article III that *the staff of correctional systems must be professionally competent and well-trained*. Community correctional systems like probation have made some progress toward this goal. There has been significant movement over the last twenty years in developing a more professional cadre of probation officers. Educational requirements have been implemented, compensation has slowly improved, and career opportunities have expanded to the point where the field of probation is able to attract some of the best and brightest young students. Unfortunately, this movement toward professionalism has not been evident within the prison systems.

There are very few other jobs in our nation that are as unappealing as that of a correctional officer. The prison guard is required to carry out the "dirty work" of society not so unlike the police officer. But the police officer works visibly among the citizens and commands a certain degree of respect. Hardly anything good can be said about the work milieu of the prison guard in most large, maximum-security prisons. The job is dangerous and boring at the same time. There are few financial and fewer intangible rewards. Manipulation and distrust are fundamental features of the prison. Emotions are stultified. Desperation and despair, hopelessness, bitterness and hostility—these are the sensations of prison life. On the matter of attracting good employees, the working conditions in prison make this nearly impossible. Even if the salaries and benefits were improved, it is unlikely that many would be attracted to this career. The most feasible method for improving corrections through personnel would seem to be from the top.

Leadership selection for correctional agencies shall be on the basis of merit . . . with tenure assured as long as there is demonstrated competent performance and compliance with professional and ethical standards (Article III-12). It could be argued that the widespread violation of this principle is the most elemental barrier to an improved prison system. The commissioners of corrections who run the prison systems are in most states appointed and serve at the pleasure of the governor, thus making them more sensitive to political than professional standards. Granted, there have been some concerned and courageous commissioners. For the most part, however, the commissioner of corrections seems destined to play the role of scapegoat in case something goes wrong in the prison bureaucracy, as usually it does. The primary functions of the commissioner are to insulate the governor from prison matters and to manage the crises just well enough that they do not become hot political issues.

In a very real sense, professional leadership is not desired within the prison systems, because it would upset the sensitive balance that allows politicians (governors, presidents, and legislators, as well as judges, sheriffs, and prosecutors) to use crime as a campaign issue without having to address the costs of harsher punishments.

We might think about the political problems that would be created if correctional personnel took active roles in advocating professional standards as the members of the educational field do. There are always various proposals for improving the educational system with sweeping changes like requiring certain test scores or extending the school year to eleven months. But the superintendents, school principal associations, and teacher unions will always demand to know the costs of such changes and the sources of revenues to fund new programs and policies. Good pieces of educational legislation are often tabled because of the lack of funding to maintain professional standards regarding teacher-to-student ratios, per capita spending levels, etc. In corrections, these checks and balances do not exist. Widespread changes in the criminal law have taken place throughout the nation over the last decade, with dramatic consequences for prison administrators, but there was only minimal input and little consideration of the views of those who had to deal with the changes. Now, after the fact, states are beginning to have to grapple with the unmanageable strains that have been put on state budgets by the ballooning increases in prison populations. Prison officials are seldom heard from again and still have little input into the major decisions that affect their domain.

Another serious problem arising from the lack of professionalism and effective leadership in corrections is the dearth of information about prisons and prisoners. As prison problems have become more serious, access to the institutions and to records and data has become more limited. Under the guise of security, prison officials have made it more and more difficult for researchers, the media, and concerned citizens to gather information about prison operations. While nearly every other public agency is subject to intense scrutiny and evaluation, correctional departments provide only the barest of data for public consumption. Many of the most basic questions about prisons and prisoners remain unanswered because of the difficulties in carrying out research on prison matters. Correctional officials could improve this situation significantly by adhering to article IV of the ACA principles: *Correctional agencies have a continuing responsibility to promote, sponsor and participate in research and program evaluation efforts.*

The review of American Correctional Association principles illustrates that sound philosophies and professional standards have been in place throughout most of the history of our nation's prison systems. The question then becomes one of figuring out why prison systems have been unable to live up to their own basic ideals. In the final section we will attempt to address this question by examining the kinds of changes that will be necessary in order to facilitate meaningful reform in the field of corrections. It is important to remember that prison reform will not occur simply because of new and innovative ideas. As we have seen throughout the book, the ideas already exist. The task is to explore ways of implementing some of the ideas, which is likely to take place only when certain first steps have been taken. Several things must happen before we can begin to think seriously about improving the effectiveness of our prisons.

Antecedents to Change

1. The Empowerment of Corrections. Within the executive branch of government, the most basic prerequisite for changing prisons is to disengage correctional officials from the political patronage system. There can be little question that correctional departments are among the weakest organizations in terms of having control over their own destiny when commissioners serve at the pleasure of the governors. It is nearly impossible to carry out any kind of meaningful planning when organizations have control over neither the numbers of people they will have to serve nor the resources that they will be given. In order to make the field of corrections more professional, there needs to be a willingness to allow all personnel a greater voice in the matters that affect their work environment. One trademark of a profession is that it has the power to influence policy decisions that are made regarding the nature and quality of the work situation.

An initial step in this direction would begin with correctional officer unions. Upper-level management (i.e., deputy wardens, wardens, and commissioners) cannot be expected to take a strong stance against politically unpopular issues like overcrowding if the front-line officers continue to accept worse and worse working conditions. Correctional administrators must feel the pressure from below. They need to understand fully the burdens that are placed on guards as conditions deteriorate. To a certain degree, of course, prison guards are also imprisoned (see Lombardo, 1981). It often appears that governors and legislators are unaware of the actual conditions in the prisons, and they tend to forget that it is not only the inmates who have to spend time inside the walls, but also the correctional staff and officers. There may not be much concern or sympathy for the inmate; however, it is irresponsible to ignore the working conditions of public employees, especially when they are exposed to increasingly dangerous situations.

The American Correctional Association will also need to support the guard unions. As with any professional association, the ACA is responsible for setting minimal standards that allow employees to function in a workable environment. The National Educational Association, for example, has worked long and hard to convince legislators and the public that teacher-student ratios cannot exceed certain limits if education is expected to be effective. The ACA has developed minimal standards and guidelines in the past, but the problem is that they have not been forceful enough in insisting that the standards be followed. In corrections, there has been a tendency toward the "management by crisis" mentality, whereby larger numbers of inmates are readily accepted with the *hope* that additional funding might be forthcoming. Professionalism will become a reality in corrections only when administrators and guards begin to demand that they receive the consideration and support necessary to carry out their jobs in an effective manner.

2. Segregation of the Nonviolent Offender. Until we are able to accept noninstitutional alternatives for the handling of nonviolent offenders, every effort must be made to segregate this group from the more violent groups of prisoners. It is clearly in the best interest of society to guarantee that the nonviolent offender will not be subjected to the degradation and brutalization that is now commonplace in maximum-security prisons. Because of the relatively short sentences they receive, the nonviolent offender needs to be prepared for reentry into society early in the prison stay. Care needs to be taken that this group does not become completely "prisonized" and develop values and attitudes that make them *more* of a threat to society when they are released. This can be accomplished by creating a normalized atmosphere within a more open prison setting that is conducive to the nonviolent offenders maintaining family

and social ties. In this kind of setting, where staff and inmates are not terrorized by the constant threat posed by violent prisoners, there can evolve a trust between staff and inmates that improves the chance that something positive will take place during the prison sentence.

The judicial branch can play a major role in accomplishing this objective. Appellate court judges have become sensitized to the problems of housing violent and nonviolent offenders together through the 1983 suits discussed in chapter 2. However, it is the trial court judges who are able to address this matter more directly by becoming more knowledgeable about the prison systems. Trial court judges often recommend that an offender serve his sentence in a particular kind of correctional institution, but placement by the department of corrections usually depends on the availability of bed space. By insisting that nonviolent offenders be placed in less harsh institutions, the sentencing judges can provide impetus for correctional organizations to redefine the roles of specific institutions within their system. This type of coordination between the judiciary and corrections is a precursor to any meaningful change in how we use the sanctions of short- and long-term imprisonment.

3. One Prisoner Per Cell. Within the legislative branch of government, the one most important step to be taken toward improving prisons is to require that we "pay as we go" by adopting the "one prisoner per cell" concept. The runaway prison populations are the result of abandoning the idea that each inmate is required to have his or her own cell. No state would consider allowing such dramatic increases in prison populations if it had to pay for the construction of new cells for all new inmates. Prior to the last decade, it was generally viewed as unsound penological practice to house more than one prisoner in a cell. There was a theoretical, a legal, and a practical reason behind this belief. Theoretically, there was the refinement of the old principle of "penitence," changed today to mean that the inmate needed some degree of privacy and solitude in order to "get it together." In the legal sense, states were and are required to provide protection for those they incarcerate, and placing more than one person in a cell precludes the guarantee of safety. The practical reason for maintaining populations at the rated capacity level was that it made the work environment in

prisons almost bearable. We know now that abandoning the "one person per cell" principle has made the prisons unsafe, unclean, ineffective, and almost unworkable.

4. Integration of Probation and Prison Systems. One of the most troubling aspects of the prison overcrowding crisis is that it has happened at the same time that probation and community corrections have expanded and improved. Many new probation services and community agencies have sprung up in recent years, and these programs have attracted some of the most educated and professional new members of the corrections field. However, the growth of these endeavors has been dwarfed by the gargantuan increases in prison budgets. One major reason for this imbalance has to do with the organizational structure in corrections. Since the prison systems and community corrections are typically separate organizations, there is little planning and coordination between them. In fact, prison officials may even see probation and community corrections as a threat. This is probably why we so rarely hear commissioners call for a wider use of probation as a partial solution to their overcrowding problems.

In order to develop a systematic scheme of legal punishments and a better organized system of corrections, we must overcome the fragmentation and competition that has traditionally characterized the field. While some states have an integrated system of corrections, there is typically little communication and support among the various correctional agencies within a state. A systematic and graduated scale of legal sanctions requires that mechanisms be in place to allow the movement of offenders from one phase of corrections to another in a rational manner. Much of the criticism of corrections results from the fact that one component does not know what the other is doing. This problem is particularly acute with regard to the two broad subfields of institutional and community corrections. Probation and community corrections will continue to be ignored until they are able to join forces with prison departments or establish an organizational arrangement of their own that is on equal footing with the prison systems.

5. Rethinking Crime and Punishment. Prospects for an improved system of corrections and a moderation of punishment are not good until our popular notions about crime and punishment are modified. How these changes in attitudes might come about is

complex. We cannot, however, overlook the two omnipresent sources of social values and attitudes—politicians and the media. The politicization and dramatization of crime by politicians and the media continue to generate feelings and beliefs that run counter to attempts at formulating reasoned and moderate crime control policies. Since the 1960s politicians have exploited the crime issue by ignoring the conditions that are related to crime and espousing simplistic and unrealistic solutions. They have long since recognized the emotional appeal of "get tough" rhetoric, which is particularly captivating when the social and financial costs are left unspoken.

Similarly, media sources have become more and more allured by the marketability of glorified crime stories. Under the guise of the public's right to know, television in particular has produced a wide assortment of nightly shows that sensationalize the most unusual and uncommon crime stories. This voyeuristic form of "tabloid journalism" seems to thrive on providing unnerving glimpses into the lurid details of personal tragedies with no concern for the people involved and no attempt to explore the real issues. The print media also tends to emphasize those cases in which the crime and/or the outcome are particularly heinous, bizarre, engrossing, or incredulous. Of major concern regarding these practices is the hardening of attitudes that seems likely to take place. Without some type of balance in portraying the crime picture, it is not surprising that citizens grossly overestimate the extent of violent crime. Crime control policies are often based on these very inaccurate perceptions. Furthermore, it is not unexpected that the public will view the justice system as ineffective and bungling when news reports gloss over the ever present complexities of administering justice in a democratic society.

It is perhaps most important for us to remember that prisons are indeed a reflection of society. Prison systems are likely to be improved only as we move toward a society that is truly "a kinder and gentler nation." Many of our present policy directives seem to be toward a meaner and harsher nation. Crime control policies that ignore the problems of unemployment, homelessness, poverty, discrimination, inadequate health care, and unequal education can only result in a justice system and prisons that are in a continual state of crisis. When social conditions are neglected and deteriorate to the point where many are living on the fringes of society, the justice system cannot and should not be expected to deal with the intractable problems of social injustice. As the prison systems are filled with more and more individuals who have little hope for the future, the justice system will become even less "successful" with more recidivism, and the cycle will continue.

Prisons ARE a measure of a society's civility. When all members of society are not shown respect and compassion in a general sense, the prisons will certainly not exhibit these qualities. As we have seen, nations like Denmark that have been successful in developing better prison systems are those in which the basic needs of all citizens have been addressed. To discuss prison reform in the absence of plans for broader social reform is futile. The many ideas presented here and elsewhere for improving prisons will come to have meaning only to the extent that they are part of a more comprehensive plan to achieve social justice. This is not to say that discussion and debate about prison reform should not continue, however. With regard to the nonviolent offender, it is especially important to reiterate and reemphasize the inappropriateness and counterproductive nature of lengthy sentences to large, closed, maximum-security prisons. Attention must continue to be focused on this matter.

In conclusion, prisons in crisis are indicative of the basic dilemma faced by society. Each society must continually decide whether it will treat the least fortunate citizens with compassion and opportunity or with scorn and punishment. It is one thing to talk about individual responsibilities and obligations when the social structure provides adequate avenues for success. It is quite another matter to demand higher standards of behavior when there is little hope of achievement and few opportunities for success. Too often, the debates about crime and crime control concentrate on different methods of *reacting* to criminal behavior. Taking a more proactive approach to crime prevention means that the emphasis is shifted toward a recognition of the social problems and living conditions that are related to crime. Prisons and legal sanctions generally become more unnecessary as society begins to minimize that proportion of crime that results from lack of opportunity and desperation. Social justice is more important in a society than criminal justice. Opportunity is as necessary as responsibility. And hope is certainly more beneficial than fear.

Epilogue

Let us end with a most interesting comment on the role of criminologists and all other citizens in the undertaking known as prison reform. It is time for a change.

> During the past ten years, particularly those of the Reagan admin-istration, realism has become de rigueur. By this term is meant that planners and citizens act as if they are encountering a limited range of possibilities, from which an exit is unlikely. "Crack pot realism" is the phrase used by C. Wright Mills to describe this condition. As part of this realism, enthusiasm about reform is es-chewed. To be a reformer and call for experimentation is consid-ered to be naive, or indicative of someone who has not recovered fully from the 1960's. . . . prison reform will not make any pro-gress until the facade of realism is undermined. This trend has been perpetrated as a result of the emphasis that has been placed on technical expertise, science, cybernetics, and other similar means employed to increase efficiency . . . as long as a world view prevails that elevates economy in importance, only technical fixes will be tolerated. New assumptions about reality must be spawned, so that creativity is not subverted by pragmaticism. But . . . creating reality is not imagined to be a proper activity for a scientist. Therefore, as long as criminologists and sociologists limit themselves in this way, prison reform will be left to techno-crats or politicians. Why should this be accepted, for these bu-reaucrats are not value-free. Hence, sociologists and criminologists should not be afraid to introduce different values into discussions about the missions of prisons. In this way, the de-bate over prison reform can be expanded, which is a maneuver that clearly will be productive. (Murphy and Dison, 1990, pp. 163–73)

Whether scientist or citizen, different values and creative ideas will be the building blocks of a successful prison reform movement. We will continue to live with the disgrace of today's prisons until a new reality is in place.

References

1. The Sentence of Imprisonment

Austin, James, and Tillman, Robert. 1988. *Ranking the Nation's Most Punitive States*. San Francisco: National Council on Crime and Delinquency.

Bailey, William; Martin, David; and Gray, Louis. 1974. "Crime and Deterrence: A Correctional Analysis." *Journal of Research in Crime and Delinquency* 11: 124–43.

Beck, Alan, and Shipley, Bernard. 1987. *Recidivism of Young Parolees*. Washington, D.C.: Bureau of Justice Statistics.

Becker, Gary. 1968. "Crime and Punishment: An Economic Approach." *Journal of Political Economy* 76: 174–82.

Becker, Howard S. 1979. *Outsiders*. New York: Macmillan, 1963.

Biles, David. "Crime and the Use of Prison." *Federal Probation* 43: 39–42.

Blumstein, Alfred; Cohen, Jacqueline; and Nagen, Daniel. 1978. *Deterrence and Incapacitation*. Washington, D.C.: National Academy of Science.

Carroll, Leo, and Doubet, Mary Beth. 1983. "U.S. Social Structure and Imprisonment." *Criminology* 21: 449–56.

Chambliss, William J. 1964. "A Sociological Analysis of the Law of Vagrancy." *Social Problems* 12: 67–77.

Chappell, Duncan. 1988. "International Developments in Corrections." *The Prison Journal* 68: 34–40.

Chiricos, Theodore G., and Waldo, Gordon P. 1970. "Punishment and Crime: An Examination of Some Evidence." *Social Problems* 18: 200–17.

Davis, James F. 1952. "Crime News in Colorado Newspapers." *American Journal of Sociology* 57: 325–30.

Doleschal, Eugene. 1977. "Rate and Length of Imprisonment." *Crime and Delinquency* 23: 51–58.

Ehrlich, Isaac. 1975. "The Deterrent Effect of Capital Punishment: A Question of Life and Death." *American Economic Review* 65: 397–417.

Fishman, Mark. 1978. "Crime Waves as Ideology." *Social Problems* 26: 531–43.

Forst, Brian E. 1976. "Participation in Illegitimate Activities: Further Empirical Findings." *Policy Analysis*: 477–92.

Fox, Vernon. 1977. *Community-Based Corrections.* Englewood Cliffs, N.J.: Prentice-Hall.

Garfinkel, Harold. 1956. "Conditions of Successful Degradation Ceremonies." *American Journal of Sociology* 61: 421–22.

Garofalo, James. 1978. "Radical Criminology and Criminal Justice: Points of Divergence and Contact." *Crime and Social Justice* 10: 17–28.

Gilman, David. 1975. "The Sanction of Imprisonment." *Crime and Delinquency* 21: 337–47.

Gottfredson, Stephen D., and Taylor, Ralph B. 1984. "Public Policy and Prison Populations." *Judicature* 68: 190–201.

Greene, Jack R., and Bynum, Tim S. 1982. "T.V. Crooks: Implications of Latent Role Models for Theories of Delinquency." *Journal of Criminal Justice* 10: 177–90.

Innes, Christopher. 1988. *Profile of State Prison Inmates.* Washington D.C.: Bureau of Justice Statistics.

Jankovic, Ivan. 1977. "Labor Market and Imprisonment." *Crime and Social Justice* 8: 17–31.

Kitsuse, John I., and Cicourel, Aaron V. 1963. "A Note on the Use of Official Statistics." *Social Problems* 11: 131–39.

Lindren, Sue. 1987. *Justice Expenditures and Employment, 1985.* Washington, D.C.: Bureau of Justice Statistics.

Lofland, John. 1966. *Deviance and Identity.* Englewood Cliffs, N.J.: Prentice-Hall.

Logan, Charles H. 1972. "General Deterrent of Imprisonment." *Social Forces* 51: 64–73.

Matza, David. 1964. *Delinquency and Drift.* New York: John Wiley.

McGarrell, Edmund F. 1988. *Juvenile Correctional Reform.* Albany: State University of New York Press.

———. 1991. "Institutional Theory and the Stability of a Conflict Model of the Imprisonment Rate." Unpublished paper.

Mitford, Jessica. 1973. *Kind and Usual Punishment.* New York: Knopf.

Mullin, Joan. 1980. *American Prisons and Jails.* Washington, D.C.: U.S. Department of Justice.

Murton, Tom, and Hyams, Joe. 1969. *Accomplices to Crime: The Arkansas Prison Scandal.* New York: Grove Press.

National Council on Crime and Delinquency. 1975. "News and Notes." *Crime and Delinquency* 21: 391–402.

Packer, Herbert L. 1968. *The Limits of the Criminal Sanction.* Palo Alto, Calif.: Stanford University Press.

Pepinsky, Harold E. 1980. *Crime Control Strategies.* New York: Oxford University Press.

Platt, Anthony M. 1969. *The Child Savers.* Chicago: University of Chicago Press.

Pogue, Thomas F. 1975. "Effect of Police Expenditures on Crime Rates: Some Evidence." *Public Finance Quarterly* 3: 14–44.

Quinney, Richard. 1970. *The Social Reality of Crime.* Boston: Little, Brown.

Rector, Milton G. 1975. "The Extravagance of Imprisonment." *Crime and Delinquency* 21: 323–30.

Schur, Edwin M. 1980. "Can the 'Old' and 'New' Criminologies Be Reconciled?" In *Radical Criminology,* ed. James A. Inciardi. Beverly Hills: Sage.

Schwendinger, Julia, and Schwendinger, Herman. 1980. "The New Idealism and Penal Living Standards." *Crime and Social Justice* 13: 45–54.

Selke, William L. 1980. "The Impact of Higher Education on Crime Ideologies." *Journal of Criminal Justice* 8: 175–84.

Selke, William L., and Andersson, Steen A. 1992. "A Model for Ranking the Punitiveness of the States." *Journal of Quantitative Criminology* 8: 217–32.

Senna, Joseph J., and Siegel, Larry J. 1990. *Introduction to Criminal Justice.* St. Paul: West.

Silberman, Charles. 1980. *Criminal Violence, Criminal Justice.* New York: Vintage.

Sjoquist, David. 1973. "Property Crime and Economic Behavior: Some Empirical Results." *American Economic Review* 63: 439–46.

Smykla, John Ortiz. 1981. *Community-Based Corrections: Concepts and Strategies.* New York: Macmillan.

Solomon, Hassim M. 1976. *Community Corrections.* New York: John Wiley.

Sutherland, Edwin H. 1949. *White-Collar Crime.* New York: Holt, Rinehart, and Winston.

Tittle, Charles R. 1969. "Crime Rates and Legal Sanctions." *Social Problems* 16: 409–13.

———. 1980. *Sanctions and Social Deviance.* New York: Praeger.

Tittle, Charles R., and Logan, C. H. 1973. "Sanctions and Deviance: Evidence and Remaining Questions." *Law and Society Review* 7: 371–92.

U.S. Department of Justice. 1989. *Prisoners in State and Federal Institutions.* Washington, D.C.: Government Printing Office.

Waller, Irvin, and Chan, Janet. 1974. "Prison Use: A Canadian and International Comparison." *Criminal Law Quarterly* 17: 47–71.

Zimmerman, Sherwood E.; VanAlstyne, David J.; and Dunn, Christopher. 1988. "The National Punishment Survey and Public Policy Consequences." *Journal of Research in Crime and Delinquency* 25: 120–49.

Zimring, Franklin E., and Hawkins, Gordon. 1991. *The Scale of Imprisonment.* Chicago: University of Chicago Press.

2. U.S. Prisons in the Nineties

Atkins, Burton, and Pogrebin, Mark. 1978. *The Invisible Justice System.* Cincinnati: Anderson.

Braithwaite, John. 1982. "Challenging 'Just Deserts.'" *Journal of Criminal Law and Criminology* 73 (Summer): 723–63.

Brewer, David; Beckett, Gerald; and Holt, Norman. 1981. "Determinate Sentencing in California." *Journal of Research in Crime and Delinquency* 18: 201–31.

Cahalan, Margaret. 1979. "Trends in Incarceration in the U.S. since 1880." *Crime and Delinquency* 25: 9–41.

Casper, Jonathan; Brereton, David; and Neal, David. 1983. "The California Determinate Sentencing Law." *Criminal Law Bulletin* 19: 405–33.

Clear, Todd; Hewitt, John; and Regoli, Robert. 1978. "Discretion and the Determinate Sentence: Its Distribution, Control and Effect on Time Served." *Crime and Delinquency* 24: 428–45.

Collins, William C. 1986. *Correctional Law 1986*. College Park, Md.: American Correctional Association.

Davies, Malcolm. 1985. "Determinate Sentencing Reform in California and Its Impact on the Penal System." *British Journal of Criminology* 25: 1–30.

Dershowitz, Alan. 1976. *Fair and Certain Punishment*. New York: McGraw-Hill.

Doleschal, Eugene. 1979. "Crime—Some Popular Beliefs." *Crime and Delinquency* 25: 1–8.

Federal Bureau of Investigation. 1989. *Uniform Crime Report - 1988*. Washington, D.C.: U.S. Government Printing Office.

Fogel, David. 1975. *We Are the Living Proof*. Cincinnati: Anderson.

Gaes, Gerald G., and McGuire, William. 1985. "Prison Violence: The Contribution of Crowding versus Other Determinants of Prison Assault Rates." *Journal of Research in Crime and Delinquency* 22: 41–65.

Giari, Maygene. 1979. "In Oklahoma, Building More Prisons Has Solved No Problems." *Crime and Delinquency* 25: 9–41.

Goodstein, Lynne, et al. 1984. *Determinate Sentencing and the Correctional Process*. Washington, D.C.: U.S. Government Printing Office.

Greenberg, David F., and Humphries, Drew. 1980. "The Cooptation of Fixed Sentencing Reform." *Crime and Delinquency* 26: 206–25.

Kerper, Hazel B., and Kerper, Janeen. 1974. *Legal Rights of the Convicted*. St. Paul: West.

Knapp, Kay. 1984. "What Sentencing Reform in Minnesota Has and Has Not Accomplished." *Judicature* 68: 181–89.

Lagoy, Steven; Hussey, Frederick; and Kramer, John. 1978. "A Comparative Assessment of Determinate Sentencing in the Four Pioneer States." *Crime and Delinquency* 24: 335–400.

Le Francois, Arthur G. 1978. "An Examination of a Desert-Based Presumptive Sentence Schedule." *Journal of Criminal Justice* 6: 35–46.

Mann, Coramae. 1989. "Random Thoughts on the Ongoing Wilbanks-Mann Discourse." *The Critical Criminologist* 1: 3–4.

Mathiesen, Thomas. 1991. *Prison on Trial*. London: Sage.

National Advisory Commission on Criminal Justice Standards and Goals.

1973. *Corrections.* Washington, D.C.: U.S. Government Printing Office.

Reiss, Albert. 1974. "Discretionary Justice in the United States." *International Journal of Criminology and Penology 2.*

Robin, Gerald D. 1987. *Introduction to the Criminal Justice System.* New York: Harper and Row.

Thomas, C. 1980. "The Impotence of Correctional Law." In *Legal Rights of Prisoners,* ed. Geoffrey Alpert. Beverly Hills: Sage. Pp. 243–60.

U.S. Department of Justice. 1989. *Prisoners in State and Federal Institutions - 1988.* Washington, D.C.: U.S. Government Printing Office.

Van den Haag, Ernest. 1974. *Punishing Criminals.* New York: Basic.

Von Hirsch, Andrew. 1977. *Doing Justice: The Choice of Punishment.* New York: Hill and Wang.

Wilson, James Q. 1975. *Thinking about Crime.* New York: Basic.

Zimring, Frank, and Hawkins, Gordon. 1973. *Deterrence.* Chicago: University of Chicago Press.

Cases

Bell v. Wolfish, 441 U.S. 562, 99 S.Ct. 1861, 60 L. Ed. 2d 447 (1979).

Cruz v. Beto, 92 S.Ct. 1079 (1972).

Estelle v. Gamble, 429 U.S. 97, 97 S.Ct. 285, 50 L. Ed. 2d 251 (1976).

Ex Parte Hull, 312 U.S. 546 (1941).

French v. Owens, 777 F.2d 1250 (7 Cir. 1985).

Fulwood v. Clemmer, 206 F.Supp. 370 (1962).

Gates v. Collier, 501 F.2d 1291 (5 Cir. 1974).

Holt v. Sarver, 309 F.Supp. 362 (1970).

Hutto v. Finney, 437 U.S. 678 (1978).

Jackson v. Bishop, 404 F.2d 571 (8 Cir. 1968).

Johnson v. Avery, 393 U.S. 483, 89 S.Ct. 747, 21 L. Ed. 2d 718 (1969).

Jordan v. Fitzharris, 257 F.Supp. 674 (1966).

Newman v. Alabama, 349 F.Supp. 278 (1972).

Nolan v. Fitzpatrick, 451 F.2d 545 (1 Cir. 1971).

Procunier v. Martinez, 416 U.S. 396, 94 S.Ct. 1800, 40 L. Ed. 2d 224 (1974).

Rhodes v. Chapman, 452 U.S. 337, 101 S.Ct. 2392, 69 L. Ed. 2d 59 (1981).

Robinson v. California, 370 U.S. 660, 82 S.Ct. 1417, 8 L. Ed. 2d 758 (1962).

Trop v. Dulles, 356 U.S. 86, 78 S.Ct. 590, 2 L. Ed. 2d 630 (1957).

Wolff v. McDonnell, 418 U.S. 539 (1974).

3. Scandinavian Criminology and Prisons

Andenaes, Johannes. 1975. "General Prevention Revisited—Research and Policy Implications." *Journal of Criminal Law and Criminology 66.*

Andersen, Erik. 1986. Interview with author. October.

Andersen, Ole E. 1985. *Ofre for vold og overvold i Danmark, 1971–84.* Copenhagen: Justitsministeriet.

Anttila, Inkeri. 1983. "Control without Repression." In *Criminal Justice in Denmark,* ed. Jorn Vestergaard. Copenhagen: International Study Program. Pp. 115–20.

Anttila, Inkeri, and Tornudd, Patrik. 1980. "Reasons for Punishment." In *Crime and Crime Control in Scandinavia,* ed. Norman Bishop. Oslo: Scandinavian Research Council for Criminology. Pp. 48–53.

Balvig, Flemming. 1982. "Crime and Criminal Policy in a Pragmatic Society." *International Journal of the Sociology of Law* 10: 9–29.

————. 1985. "Crime in Scandinavia." In *Scandinavian Criminal Policy and Criminology,* ed. Norman Bishop. Copenhagen: Scandinavian Research Council for Criminology. Pp. 7–19.

Bondeson, Ulla. 1977. *Criminal Care in Liberty.* Stockholm: Liber Forlag.

Brydenshold, H. H. 1980. "Crime Policy in Denmark." *Crime and Delinquency* 26: 35–41.

Christiansen, Karl O. 1973. *Some Considerations on the Possibility of a Rational Criminal Policy.* Copenhagen: UNAFEI Annual Report.

Christie, Nils. 1983. "Changes in Penal Values." In *Criminal Justice in Denmark,* ed. Jorn Vestergaard. Pp. 109–15.

Genfer, Juul. 1986. Interview with author. October. Copenhagen.

Greve, Vagn; Ingstrup, Ole; Jensen, Sv. Gram; and Spencer, Martin. 1984. *The Danish System of Criminal Justice.* Copenhagen: Department of Prisons and Probation.

Hildahl, Spencer. 1979. "Danish Cultural Values and Criminal Justice Policies." Unpublished paper.

Johnson, Robert. 1987. *Hard Time.* Monterey, Calif.: Brooks/Cole.

Kriminalforsorgens Arsberetning, 1985. 1986. Copenhagen: Justitsministeriets Direktorat for Kriminalforsorgen.

Kriminalstatistik, 1981–82. 1986. Copenhagen: Danmarks Statistik.

Kriminalstatistik, 1983. 1986. Copenhagen: Danmarks Statistik.

Kyvsgaard, Britta. 1983. "Imprisonment in Denmark: Current Tendencies." In *Criminal Justice in Denmark,* ed. Jorn Vestergaard. Pp. 205–22.

Lahti, Raimo. 1985. "Current Trends in Criminal Policy in the Scandinavian Countries." In *Scandinavian Criminal Policy and Criminology,* ed. Norman Bishop. Pp. 59–73.

Mathiesen, Thomas. 1986. "The Politics of Abolition." *Contemporary Crisis* 10: 81–95.

Mead, Margaret. 1935. *Sex and Temperament in Three Primitive Societies.* New York: Dell.

Philip, Bodil. 1986. Interview with author. November. Copenhagen.

Selke, William. 1985. "Judicial Management of Prisons?" *The Prison Journal* 65: 26–37.

Snare, Annika, and Bondeson, Ulla. 1985. "Criminological Research in Scandinavia." *Crime and Justice - An Annual Review of Research* 6: 231–59.

Snortum, John R., and Bodal, Kare. 1985. "Conditions of Confinement within Security Prisons: Scandinavia and California." *Crime and Delinquency* 31: 573–600.

Sourcebook of Criminal Justice Statistics. 1986. Albany, N.Y.: School of Criminal Justice.

Sveri, Knut. 1980. "Violence in Scandinavia." In *Crime and Crime Control in Scandinavia,* ed. Norman Bishop. Pp. 16–24.

Swedish Council's Working Group for Criminal Policy. 1978. *A New Penal System—Ideas and Proposals.* Stockholm: National Swedish Council for Crime Prevention.

Taylor, Erik. 1986. Interview with author. October. Copenhagen.

Umbreit, Mark S. 1980. *Crime and Punishment in Denmark.* Valparaiso, Ind.: PACT.

Uniform Crime Reports, 1983. 1984. Washington, D.C.: Federal Bureau of Investigation.

Vestergaard, Jorn. 1983. "Criminal Justice in Denmark: Key Data." In *Criminal Justice in Denmark,* ed. Jorn Vestergaard. Pp. 120–27.

Ward, David. 1979. "The Middle Way to Prison Reform." In *Prisons—Present and Possible,* ed. Marvin Wolfgang. Lexington, Mass.: Lexington.

Winslow, Jacob. 1986. "The Drug Problem: Some Sociological Reflections on Danish Sociology's Response." *Scandinavian Studies in Criminology* 8.

Wolf, Preben. 1983. "The Effects of Prison on Criminality." In *Criminal Justice in Denmark,* ed. Jorn Vestergaard. Pp. 78–90.

4. Open versus Closed Prisons

Balvig, Flemming. 1982. "Crime and Criminal Policy in a Pragmatic Society." *International Journal of the Sociology of Law* 10: 9–29.

Bondeson, Ulla. 1981. "Criminal Care in Liberty." In *Scandinavian-Polish Workmeeting.* Copenhagen: Scandinavian Research Council for Criminology. Pp. 190–202.

Bowker, Lee. 1980. *Prison Victimization.* New York: Elsevier Press.

Christie, Nils. 1983. "Changes in Penal Values." In *Criminal Justice in Denmark,* ed. Jorn Vestergaard. Copenhagen: International Study Program. Pp. 109–15.

Clemmer, Donald. 1940. *The Prison Community.* New York: Holt, Rinehart, and Winston.

Conrad, John. 1966. "Violence in Prison." *Annals of the American Academy of Political and Social Science* 364: 113–19.

Crouch, Ben, and Marquart, James W. 1989. *An Appeal to Justice: Litigated Reform of Texas Prisons.* Austin: University of Texas Press.

Currie, Elliot. 1987. "Social Policy and the Future of Criminal Justice." *The Prison Journal* 67: 19–27.

Davidson, R. Theodore. 1974. *Chicano Prisoners—The Key to San Quentin*. New York: Holt, Rinehart, and Winston.

Downes, David. 1988. *Contrasts in Tolerance: Post-War Penal Policies in The Netherlands and England and Wales*. London: Oxford University Press.

Goffman, Erving. 1961. *Asylums*. Garden City, N.Y.: Anchor.

Goodstein, Lynne. 1979. "Inmate Adjustment to Prison and the Transition to Community Life." *Journal of Research in Crime and Delinquency* 16: 246–75.

Harris, Kay. 1987. "Moving into the New Millennium—Toward a Feminist Vision of Justice." *The Prison Journal* 67: 27–39.

Heckscher, Stan. 1981. "Conditions and Rules of Imprisonment." In *Scandinavian-Polish Workmeeting*. Copenhagen: Scandinavian Research Council for Criminology. Pp. 252–69.

Irwin, John. 1985. *Jail: Managing the Underclass in American Society*. Berkeley: University of California Press.

Jones, Howard, and Cornes, Paul. 1977. *Open Prisons*. London: Routledge and Kegan Paul.

Karraker, Naneen. 1987. "Banishing Goodness and Badness—Toward a New Penology." *The Prison Journal* 67: 49–54.

Kauffman, Kelsey. 1988. *Prison Officers and Their World*. Cambridge: Harvard University Press.

Lahti, Raimo. 1981. "Deprivation of Liberty and Loss of Civil Rights." In *Scandinavian-Polish Workmeeting*. Copenhagen: Scandinavian Research Council for Criminology. Pp. 203–20.

Manocchio, Anthony J., and Dunn, Jimmy. 1982. *The Time Game: Two Views of a Prison*. Beverly Hills: Sage (2nd printing).

Mathiesen, Thomas. 1986. "The Politics of Abolition." *Contemporary Crisis* 10: 81–95.

Moczydlowski, Pawel. 1992. *The Hidden Life of Polish Prisons*. Bloomington: Indiana University Press.

Murphy, John W., and Dison, Jack E. 1990. *Are Prisons Any Better?* Newbury Park, Calif.: Sage.

Murton, Thomas O. 1976. *The Dilemma of Prison Reform*. New York: Holt, Rinehart, and Winston.

Nakell, Barry. 1977. "On Behalf of a Moratorium on Prison Construction." *Crime and Delinquency* 23: 154–72.

Orlands, Leonard. 1975. *Prisons: Houses of Darkness*. New York: Free Press.

Platek, Monika. 1981. "Criminal Care in Liberty." In *Scandinavian-Polish Workmeeting*. Copenhagen: Scandinavian Research Council for Criminology. Pp. 173–89.

Smykla, John Ortiz. 1980. *Coed Prison*. New York: Human Sciences Press.

Sykes, Gresham M. 1958. *Society of Captives*. Princeton: Princeton University Press.

Tittle, Charles; Villemez, Wayne; and Smith, Douglas. 1978. "The Myth of Social Class and Criminality." *American Sociological Review* 43: 643–46.

Wolf, Preben. 1983. "The Effects of Prison on Criminality." In *Criminal Justice in Denmark,* ed. Jorn Vestergaard. Copenhagen: International Study Program.

Zimbardo, Philip G. 1983. "Pathology of Imprisonment." In *Corrections-An Issues Approach* (2nd ed.), ed. Lawrence F. Travis III, Martin D. Schwartz, and Todd R. Clear. Cincinnati: Anderson.

5. International Corrections

Ali, Badr-El-Din. 1986. "Methodological Problems in International Criminal Justice Research." *International Journal of Comparative and Applied Criminal Justice* 10: 163–76.

Archambeault, William G., and Fenwick, Charles G. 1988. "A Comparative Analysis of Culture, Safety, and Organizational Management Factors in Japanese and U.S. Prisons." *The Prison Journal* 68: 3–24.

Ball, Richard A.; Huff, C. Ronald; and Lilly, J. Robert. 1988. *House Arrest and Corrections: Doing Time at Home.* Beverly Hills: Sage.

Bartollas, Clemens. 1990. "The Prison—Disorder Personified." In *Are Prisons Better? Twenty Years of Correctional Reform,* ed. John W. Murphy and Jack E. Dison. Newbury Park, Calif.: Sage.

Bierne, Piers. 1983. "Generalization and Its Discontents—The Comparative Study of Crime." In *Comparative Criminology,* ed. Elmer Johnson and Israel Barak-Gantz. Pasadena, Calif.: Sage.

Bottoms, A. E. 1987. "Limiting Prison Use: Experience in England and Wales." *Howard Journal* 26: 177–202.

Bowker, Lee H. 1982. *Corrections: The Art and the Science.* New York: Macmillan.

Bureau of Justice Assistance. 1989. *Electronic Monitoring in Intensive Probation and Parole Programs.* Washington, D.C.: U.S. Department of Justice.

Christie, Nils. 1970. "Comparative Criminology." *Canadian Journal of Corrections* 12: 40–46.

del Carmen, R., and Vaughn, J. 1986. "Legal Issues in Electronic Surveillance in Probation." *Federal Probation* 50: 60–69.

Douglas, Gilliam. 1984. "Dealing with Prisoners' Grievances." *British Journal of Criminology* 24: 150–67.

Downes, David. 1988. *Contrasts in Tolerance: Post-war Penal Policies in the Netherlands, and England and Wales.* London: Oxford University Press.

Fenwick, Charles R. 1982. "Crime Control in Japan: Implications for the United States." *International Journal of Comparative and Applied Criminal Justice* 6: 61–72.

Fox, Vernon. 1983. *Correctional Institutions.* Englewood Cliffs, N.J.: Prentice-Hall.

Franke, Herman. 1990. "Dutch Tolerance: Facts and Fables." *British Journal of Criminology* 30.

Friel, C. M., and Vaughn, J. B. 1986. "Consumers' Guide to Electronic Monitoring of Probationers." *Federal Probation* 50: 3–4.

Gable, R. K. 1986. "Applications of Personal Telemonitoring to Current Problems in Corrections." *Journal of Criminal Justice* 14: 431–46.

Graham, John. 1990. "Decarceration in the Federal Republic of Germany." *British Journal of Criminology* 30: 150–70.

Griffiths, Curt T. 1988. "Canadian Corrections: Policy and Practice North of 49th." *The Prison Journal* 68: 51–62.

Hornum, Finn. 1988. "Corrections in Two Social Welfare Democracies: Denmark and Sweden." *The Prison Journal* 68: 63–82.

Iacovetta, G. G. 1981. "Research Problems and Issues in Comparative Corrections." *International Journal of Comparative and Applied Criminal Justice* 5: 205–11.

Johnson, Elmer H., and Barak-Gantz, Israel L., eds. 1983. *Comparative Criminology.* Pasadena, Calif.: Sage.

Mannheim, Herman. 1965. *Comparative Criminology.* Boston: Houghton Mifflin.

McConville, Sean. 1975. "Boards of Visitors of Penal Institutions." *British Journal of Criminology* 15: 391–94.

National Institute of Justice. 1989. *Electronic Monitoring of Offenders Increases.* Washington, D.C.: U.S. Department of Justice.

Needham, H. G. 1980. "Historical Perspective on the Federal- Provincial Split in Jurisdiction in Corrections." *Canadian Journal of Criminology* 22: 298–306.

Robertson, R., and Taylor, L. 1973. *Deviance, Crime and Socio-Legal Control: Comparative Perspectives.* London: Martin Robertson.

Smykla, John Ortiz. 1990. Unpublished paper.

Solzhenitsyn, Aleksandr I. 1973. *The Gulag Archipelago.* New York: Harper and Row.

Szabo, Denis. 1975. "Comparative Criminology." *Journal of Criminal Law and Criminology* 66: 366–79.

Umbreit, Mark. 1980. "Danish Use of Prisons and Community Alternatives." *Federal Probation* 44: 24–28.

Vass, Anthony A., and Weston, Alan. 1990. "Probation Day Centres as an Alternative to Custody." *British Journal of Criminology* 30: 189–206.

Walker, D. 1987. "Are Day Centres 'Alternative Probation?'" *Social Work Today* 26: 12–13.

Walker, J.; Collier, P.; and Tarling, R. 1990. "Why Are Prison Rates in

England and Wales Higher Than in Australia?" *British Journal of Criminology* 30: 24–35.
Wu, Harry. 1991. "A Prisoner's Journey." *Newsweek* 118: 30–32.

6. Toward a Moderation of Punishment

Allen, Harry E., and Simonsen, Clifford E. 1992. *Corrections in America.* New York: Macmillan.
Bowker, Lee H. 1980. *Prison Victimization.* New York: Elsevier.
Braswell, Michael; Dillingham, Steven; and Montgomery, Reid, eds. 1985. *Prison Violence in America.* Cincinnati: Anderson.
Champion, Dean J. 1990. *Probation and Parole in the United States.* Columbus, Oh.: Merrill.
DiIulio, John J. 1987. *Governing Prisons.* New York: The Free Press.
Hawkins, Gordon. 1976. *The Prison—Policy and Practice.* Chicago: University of Chicago Press.
Irwin, John. 1980. *Prisons in Turmoil.* Boston: Little, Brown.
Johnson, Robert. 1987. *Hard Time-Understanding and Reforming the Prison.* Monterey, Calif.: Brooks/Cole.
Lombardo, Lucien X. 1981. *Guards Imprisoned: Correctional Officers at Work.* New York: Elsevier.
Morris, Norval. 1974. *The Future of Imprisonment.* Chicago: University of Chicago Press.
Murphy, John W., and Dison, Jack E. 1990. *Are Prisons Any Better? Twenty Years of Correctional Reform.* Newbury Park, Calif.: Sage.
Murton, Thomas O. 1976. *The Dilemma of Prison Reform.* New York: Praeger.
Parisi, Nicolette, ed. 1982. *Coping with Imprisonment.* Beverly Hills: Sage.
Pontell, Henry N. 1984. *A Capacity to Punish: The Ecology of Crime and Punishment.* Bloomington: Indiana University Press.
Robins, Tom. 1971. *Another Roadside Attraction.* New York: Ballantine.
Sommer, Robert. 1976. *The End of Imprisonment.* New York: Oxford University Press.
Toch, Hans. 1977. *Living in Prison: The Ecology of Survival.* New York: Free Press.
Zimring, Franklin E., and Hawkins, Gordon. 1991. *The Scale of Imprisonment.* Chicago: University of Chicago Press.

Index

WILLIAM L. SELKE is Associate Professor of Criminal Justice at Indiana University.